"This important book reminds us of Dr. King's blueprint for changing the social political economic structure of our culture and shows us how we have adopted ways of being, seeing, believing, and living that go contrary to the core message of Dr. King.

It is important that today's youth understand the gap between the annual media hype on his birthday with what Dr. King actually said. We have used the auditory splendor of his 'I Have a Dream' speech to induce a sort of hypnosis that covers up the fact that Dr. King was talking about making major changes in the social, political, and economic relationships that exist in this country; he was talking about restructuring a system that produces poverty.

Jennifer Yanco reminds us that in this speech, Dr. King spoke about America's check to its people—a check that was returned, marked 'insufficient funds.' She catalogues some of the costs to our society of failing to make sure there are sufficient funds to honor the check—in terms of housing, jobs, education, and other social goods. Jogging our memories about Dr. King can provide today's youth with guidance for rebuilding our society to focus on love and respect for one's neighbors and where we begin again to take on the challenge of creating the Beloved Community Dr. King spoke of."

—Melvin H. King, *Emeritus, Massachusetts Institute of Technology, Former Massachusetts State Representative*

D1372199

MISREMEMBERING

DR. KING

REVISITING THE LEGACY OF
MARTIN LUTHER KING JR.

JENNIFER J. YANCO

INDIANA UNIVERSITY PRESS
Bloomington & Indianapolis

This book is a publication of

Indiana University Press
Office of Scholarly Publishing
Herman B Wells Library 350
1320 East 10th Street
Bloomington, Indiana 47405 USA

iupress.indiana.edu

Telephone   800-842-6796
Fax   812-855-7931

Library of Congress Cataloging-
in-Publication Data

Yanco, Jennifer J.
  Misremembering Dr. King : revisiting the
legacy of Martin Luther King Jr. / Jennifer J. Yanco.
  pages cm
  Includes bibliographical references.
  ISBN 978-0-253-01416-0 (pb)
  ISBN 978-0-253-01424-5 (eb)
  1. King, Martin Luther, Jr., 1929-1968. 2. King,
Martin Luther, Jr., 1929-1968—Political and social
views. 3. Civil rights movements—United States—
History—20th century. 4. Nonviolence—United
States—History—20th century. 5. Civil rights
workers—United States—Biography. 6. Baptists—
United States—Clergy—Biography. I. Title.
  E185.97.K5Y36 2014
  323.092—dc23
  [B]
                                    2013050152

1 2 3 4 5   19 18 17 16 15 14

To the memory of my father,
Allan Julian Yanco, 1921–2012

A civilization can flounder as readily in the face of moral and spiritual bankruptcy as it can through financial bankruptcy.

Martin Luther King Jr., *Where Do We Go from Here: Chaos or Community?*

CONTENTS

PREFACE

THIS BOOK IS A RESPONSE to the collective amnesia about Dr. Martin Luther King Jr. The popular memory of Dr. King's leadership of the civil rights movement and his advocacy of nonviolence as a tool for social change is accurate, but there is much more to the story. Dr. King posed many challenges to us as a society; the fact that we have been unwilling to deal with them has by no means made them go away. My hope in writing this book is to revive them.

For the past dozen years or so, I've been involved in working with other white people, mainly through adult education programs, to reeducate ourselves, to reach out to others, and to find effective ways to challenge racism in our communities. I've learned an enormous amount from the people who have taken the course and from my fellows who collectively run it. Aside from the fact that most of us are white, we are an amazingly diverse group. I myself am a baby boomer who came of age in the sixties, a white American who grew up in comfortable, if modest, circumstances. My father was the child of immigrants from the southern foothills of the Tatra Mountains in Eastern Europe; his parents left home as teenagers and never returned. My mother is from a long line of rural New Englanders. When I was just four, we packed up and moved from Boston to a small town in northwest Washington State. Like hundreds of thousands of towns across the country, it was a town where white people lived; "others" were not welcome. In summers, we used to make the long drive across the

United States back to the East Coast to reconnect with the family we had left behind. It was only much later, my understanding of the world having been considerably enriched by African American friends and colleagues, that I understood that such cross-country road travel would have been very risky had we been African American. The charming little white towns along the way might not have been so charming and the motels and diners where we stayed and ate might have turned us away, or worse.

We were, I suppose, a typical white, working/middle–class family: a two-parent family with three children—I am the oldest and have a sister and a brother. My father, a craftsman and small business owner, was the sole breadwinner until my mother took a job outside the home when I was in my early teens. We lived in a college town and for a number of years supplemented the family income—and culture—by lodging Canadian college students in our home. I attended college in my home town, where I became involved in the antiwar movement and in working as an ally at the edges of the Black Power movement. I am the only one in my family to have completed college. A year or so after graduating, I joined the Peace Corps and went to teach high school in what is now the Democratic Republic of Congo. I later went on to earn a PhD in linguistics and African studies, and ten years after that, a master's in public health. Needless to say, these educational opportunities have opened many doors for me. I am mindful of the fact that my whiteness has had no small part in determining my trajectory in life. I had intimations of this early on and have spent the better part of my life trying, in one way and another, to understand this "race" privilege and the moral imperative to work toward its abolition. I've still got a long way to go, and I thank the many people who have helped me get this far.

While I was writing this book, my father passed away unexpectedly. Thinking back, I remember well his reactions to the television footage that entered our home far off in northwest Washington State during the civil rights movement. It was as if we were watching something from another country. I specifically recall watching footage of the Selma–Montgomery March and how visibly upset my father was to see such brutality directed against people who, as he put it, "had done nothing to deserve it." But like many of us—and by "us" I mean white people in the United States—he did not have the tools to understand what this had to do with him. He had been cheated of those tools by a culture that, through erasing history, rendered the systemic nature of racism invisible, located it "elsewhere," and made it somebody else's business. To paraphrase James Baldwin, he was trapped in a history he did not understand. Nor did he understand the ways in which his life was—and all our lives were—interwoven with those on the screen in the complex threads of history. Like the rest of us in that small, white town and other towns and cities across the country, this rendered him inoperative in any efforts to repair it.

Reflecting on my father's passing and making sense of his life, I began to better understand the process of memorializing. I experienced firsthand how we are immediately drawn to memories that comfort us and reassure us that we have done well by the departed. I was surprised—especially as I had been thinking of this in relation to our remembering of Martin Luther King Jr.—to find myself dwelling entirely on "happy" memories that made me feel good about my father, myself, our family, and our relationships. Yet I think that it is in engaging with the thorny details, the things that we can't tie up neatly, that we stand to learn something about ourselves and how to do a better job of being human.

ACKNOWLEDGMENTS

MY THINKING ON DR. KING and his legacy has been influenced and shaped by countless people and experiences over the years. I thank the friends and colleagues who have so generously engaged with me in discussions about Dr. King and his work and for the insights they have provided along the way. There are a few people in particular whom I would like to acknowledge for their support and assistance in preparing this manuscript. I am especially grateful to my dear friend and colleague Wendy Wilson Fall; our conversations never fail to spark new ideas and ignite creative thought. And to Mel King, who so generously took the time to read and comment on drafts, sharing his wisdom and experience and reminding me of the central importance of Dr. King's message of love. I thank my friends and colleagues from White People Challenging Racism, especially Barbara Beckwith and Xochitl Kountz, for their insights and editorial advice. I am grateful to Julia Mongo, Jackie Knight, Anna Yanco-Papa, and Edith Maxwell for their editing skills; to Jeanne Koopman for her "economist's eye" on the chapter on materialism; to Mbye Cham for reviewing specific sections and sharing his perspective on Dr. King; and to Rahmane Idrissa for reading the whole works. Finally, my thanks go to Indiana University Press and especially to Kate Caras, whose support and encouragement have been invaluable. Thank you, all.

MISREMEMBERING DR. KING

Introduction: Memory and Forgetting

MARTIN LUTHER KING JR. was one of the most important moral voices of the twentieth century. Central to his work was the question of how we treat one another. His commitment to nonviolence as a tool for social change and his courageous leadership were driven by the conviction that each of us deserves to be treated with respect and dignity.

Dr. King has become an iconic figure in the pantheon of American heroes, MLK Day is a national holiday, and we have a memorial to him on the National Mall. But what was his dream, exactly, and have we really made any progress in pursuing it? With the commemoration in 2013 of the fiftieth anniversary of the March on Washington for Jobs and Freedom, where Martin Luther King Jr. delivered his famous "I Have a Dream" speech, it is a good time to review the historical record in an attempt to re-cover a more accurate memory of what he stood for. Whether in the annual celebrations of MLK Day, or in the media coverage of the inauguration of the MLK memorial in the fall of 2011, popular memories of Dr. King are striking in their omissions. They rarely reference the antiwar activist who spoke about the dangers of increasing militarism, the man who warned against rampant materialism and advocated for a guaranteed minimum living wage for all Americans, or the man who spoke up for reparations to right the wrongs of excluding generations of African Americans from the American Dream.

His analysis of what was wrong with our society challenged deeply held values and called down the wrath of many. Dr. King asked demanding questions and proposed radical solutions. But we hear little about this Dr. King. Instead, we are left with the memory of a kindly and powerful orator who led the successful nonviolent movement for civil rights. This was a major achievement, and we do well to honor him for it. Yet we dishonor him by striking from the record his concerns for wider questions of social justice, in which all of his civil rights leadership was grounded. This reworked version of who he was robs current and future generations, born after his death, of the power of his thought as a tool for serious social change.

I write this book about Martin Luther King Jr. from the vantage point of the second term of President Barack Obama, the first black president in a country dogged by a history of persistent racial injustice. Obama's election and the overwhelming support for a black candidate generated enormous hope not only in the United States, but around the world. For many, this marked the beginning of a new age.

This book, which is meant to be a corrective to the popular memory of Dr. King, also takes a look at where we are at this moment in history, when much of his message has faded from our collective consciousness. It is my hope that this book will contribute to reversing this process of forgetting and serve to revive his urgent messages. It is meant to stand as an analysis of U.S. society in light of Dr. King's prescriptions for a better future—an analysis made at this point in time, but not only for this time.

Martin Luther King Jr.'s public life was brief: he came into the spotlight at the end of 1955, when, at the age of twenty-seven, he was asked to take on the leadership of the Montgomery Improvement Association (MIA), the group that organized the bus boycott in Montgomery, Alabama. He was assassinated thirteen years later, in 1968.

It was shortly after Dr. King began his work with the MIA that he and other leaders of the civil rights movement became, under the tutelage of Bayard Rustin, adherents of nonviolence, a strategy central to the movement and the principle that guided all of Dr. King's subsequent work for civil and human rights. In his thirteen years of public life, Dr. King delivered hundreds of speeches, and wrote books, essays, and letters that bear testimony to his stature as a thinker and courageous actor. They also bear witness to his commitment to justice and the proper means of attaining it.

Dr. King called upon us to rethink our society and the forces that threaten it. He was very clear about what those forces were: militarism, materialism, and racism—forces that he called the Giant Triplets. He spent his life urging us to take measures to rein them in so as to create a healthy and vibrant society. Yet the comforting popular memory of Dr. King bears few traces of these urgent messages.

Dr. King questioned our role as "God's military agent on earth,"[1] and urged that the United States depend more on its moral power than on its military power. Yet in the years since his death, U.S. military spending has skyrocketed; the 2011 budget for defense and security-related international activities was $718 billion.[2] Rather than work to reduce our reliance on arms and increase our investments in peaceful solutions to conflict, the United States now accounts for over 40 percent of all military spending in the world. Any hoped-for a "peace dividend" is more illusory than ever before as we continue our failed strategy of using might to make right.

Dr. King spoke of economic justice and looked to a nation where everyone would be assured of the basic necessities of food, shelter, and meaningful work. Our country has moved in the opposite direction by pursuing policies that actually promote economic inequality. As the few take greater and greater shares of the nation's wealth, hunger is on the rise, unemployment rates are close to three times what they were in 1968,[3] and more people are homeless. In 2009, on a single night in January, there were an estimated 643,000 people—more than half a million—without a home nationwide.[4]

Currently in the United States, 10 percent of the population controls 75 percent of national wealth. On the other side of the coin—consumer debt—we find that 90 percent of the population holds 73 percent of personal debt. In short, the top 10 percent of the population holds three-quarters of the wealth and one-quarter of the debt, and the bottom 90 percent of the population holds three-quarters of the debt and only one-quarter of the wealth. When nine out of ten people are struggling to make ends meet, while one is living high on the hog, there's bound to be both guilt and resentment. This kind of distribution of resources (and debts) is not conducive to a healthy society.

Finally, Dr. King warned of the corrosive power of racial injustice. He challenged the nation to address the enduring legacy of racism by investing in communities to repair centuries of neglect and exclusion. While we now see African Americans in high positions, their prominence masks the fact that for all major indicators—health, educational attainment, income, employment, housing—people of color, and in particular African Americans, fall way behind white Americans. On top of this, law enforcement, the courts, and our criminal justice system have relentlessly targeted African American communities; as a result, one in three black men is now incarcerated or otherwise under the control of the state.

We are in the midst of severe societal crises. A serious reconsideration of Dr. King and his work holds out hope for resolving them. He pointed to uncomfortable facts about our society and deep-seated institutional issues that demand institutional solutions. He challenged us to change the structures of our society and government in the interests of promoting peace, assuring economic fairness, and putting an end to racism. These are formidable challenges that require a revolution in values, putting moral principles above principles of profit and might.

Our stalwart unwillingness to engage with the issues he challenged us to face—to the point of obliterating them from our collective memory—matters. The global financial and environmental crises are wreaking havoc in the lives of millions of people in the United States and throughout the world. Our attempts to address this crisis have not been successful. This may be because the roots of this crisis are moral and spiritual and have to do with the basic questions of how we treat one another. Dr. King understood this; it was at the core of his work, which is now, more than ever, of critical importance.

THE MISAPPROPRIATION OF MEMORY

Martin Luther King Jr. has become a national hero. Countless streets in cities across the country are named after him; both a national holiday and a memorial on the National Mall have been established in his honor. These tributes to the memory of an extraordinary public figure should serve to remind us of his vision and accomplishments. But the ways in which Dr. King is remembered in the context of these public memorials are strikingly out of line with what is known about him.

These public expressions of memory promote a simplified narrative about Dr. King's life, preempting alternative narratives and forestalling further discussion. The complexity of his character and mission has been replaced by a simplistic, inaccurate, and formulaic memory that has been reinforced by the media. The holiday and memorial seem to serve as "credentials" that take the place of the painful and difficult tasks of engaging with the challenges Dr. King posed. It is as if we have somehow discharged our responsibility toward his memory by enacting these public displays, allowing us to close the chapter of his life, and relieving us of any further need to seriously engage the challenges he posed.

"Misremembering," the term I use in this book's title, suggests an intention to inaccuracy, a reworking of the historical record to suit particular ends and interests. But what ends? And whose interests? In this case, misremembering references the intention to remember only the "comfortable" parts of Dr. King's message, removing those we are not willing to deal with, believing perhaps that, by having honored an African American civil rights leader, we have overcome racism and, by extension, anything else that Dr. King spoke about.

The media have been instrumental in shaping our memory of Dr. King. The constant replaying of certain selected images and words has made them central to our public memory, edging out other images and words that may be more representative of what Dr. King stood for. We have all heard, countless times, the excerpts from Dr. King's "I Have a Dream" speech, in which he expressed hope for the day when his children would "not be judged by the color of their skin, but by the content of their character," when "little black boys and black girls will be able to join hands with little white boys and white girls as sisters and brothers." These words serve to reinforce our feeling that we have made progress; however, they do not challenge the racism that underlies all aspects of our society. In the same speech, but in words we seldom hear, Dr. King spoke pointedly about continuing racial injustice. He said:

> It is obvious today that America has defaulted on this promissory note insofar as her citizens of color are concerned. Instead of honoring this sacred obligation, America has given the Negro people a bad check, a check which has come back marked "insufficient funds." But we refuse to believe that the bank of justice is bankrupt. We refuse to believe that there are insufficient funds in the great vaults of opportunity of this nation. So we have come to cash this check—a check that will give us upon demand the riches of freedom and the security of justice.[5]

Dr. King gave this speech at the March on Washington in 1963. However, few people now are aware of the fact that it was actually called the March for Jobs and Freedom, and that marchers had come from far and wide for one reason: to demand their fair share of their country's wealth and opportunity, to cash their check of justice.

Images of Dr. King in the context of civil rights movement in the South—the Montgomery bus boycott, the Birmingham Campaign, and the Selma to Montgomery march—have become part of the popular visual narrative. Other images of equally important points in his life have not. We rarely see images of Dr. King at antiwar rallies in New York or Chicago, where he spoke out forcefully against the government's military engagements. We are rarely shown images of Dr. King in the Los Angeles neighborhood of Watts, nor do we hear him decrying the economic conditions and police brutality in the African American community that provoked the rebellion there and in other cities across the nation.

Our collective memories of Dr. King permit us to claim that we honor him, while at the same time erasing and thereby dismissing his overriding concerns. Many of these concerns—like his fundamental belief that we ought to focus on how we treat one another—are hard for us to remember. This is particularly true now when the prevailing moral code seems to be "each man for himself." Internationally, the lack of concern for the well-being of others underlies our growing belligerence and widespread use of militarily condoned violence. Genuine concern for other human beings and their predicaments—the desire and ability to imagine oneself in another's place, or compassion—has been edged out by a value system that elevates the individual at the expense of the community. Not surprisingly, progress in eliminating poverty, injustice, and war has ground to a halt. If we allowed ourselves to think—to really think—about those living in poverty in our cities and rural areas, those victimized by our wars overseas, and those caught up in our criminal justice system, what changes would we want to make?

Dr. King and his memory have been done a great violence by the silencing of his full voice. We use this popular memory as reinforcement for our national illusion of progress and not, as he intended, as a guide for pursuing a more just society. Unfortunately, the memory we are left with has few traces of Dr. King's most urgent messages: that we deal with and correct the legacy of slavery that infuses all of our institutions today; that we turn away from increasing militarism as a solution to the enduring problems we face in living together in a complex world; that we find ways of assuring a more equitable distribution of opportunity and resources. The legacy of Dr. King that is taught in schools and frequently invoked on Martin Luther King Day does not seriously engage these issues. Most people, when asked, have no idea that "Giant Triplets" refers to Dr. King's formulation of the three biggest threats to our society and our world. This popular memory of Dr. King fuels self-deception and is a source of complacency.

We should ask ourselves whose beliefs would be called into question by a more accurate recollection of Dr. King's message: Who would be made uncomfortable, and whose worldview would be upset? Who, finally, gets to decide what is remembered or forgotten? The mainstream media has surely played a major role in manipulating the memory of Dr. King, but not without our silent consent. Corporations that fund the media through advertising are extremely sensitive to public tastes and desires. Programming that does not appeal to the public is quickly removed from circulation. If we continue to be served a watered-down version of Dr. King's life, it is at least partially because we have not questioned it and demanded otherwise.

Dr. King's message about the dangers of militarism, materialism, and racism make many of us squirm. It reminds us of the changes we could have made, but chose not to. It calls our attention to the ethos that has become exaggerated over the last several decades—one that deems it acceptable to have societal resources concentrated in a few hands while increasing numbers of people are unable to make ends meet, one that underlies growing military aggression, and one that undergirds a "colorblind" society where racism nevertheless continues unabated. The ways in which we remember Dr. King have facilitated these unfortunate developments by diverting our attention from the core of his message, a message that, if we heeded it—as we did briefly into the 1970s—might guide us to creating a more livable society.

In his introduction to the 2010 edition of Dr. King's fourth book, *Where Do We Go from Here: Chaos or Community?*, Vincent Harding asked, "Will Obama really see King?"[6] On this question, the jury is still out. But it is not just Barack Obama who must really see King; if things are to change, we all must. My objective in writing this book is to highlight the important aspects of Dr. King's work that have all but disappeared from popular memory, so that more of us can "really see King."

Memory is a potent force: recovering the memory of Dr. King may be a first step toward building a compassionate society that truly honors his memory. This book begins with "What We Remember," looking at the Dr. King whom we celebrate on Martin Luther King Day and through his national memorial. The next section, "What We Forget," looks at the Dr. King who is absent from the popular narrative. In it, I address each of the three major issues he emphasized in his speeches and writings: militarism, materialism, and racism. It is my hope that this book will serve as a corrective to the popular memory of Dr. King and encourage readers to seek out his writings and listen to his speeches.

The works I have drawn upon in writing this book are readily available online and in public libraries across the country. Unless otherwise noted, all quotations attributed to Dr. King are drawn from his 1968 book, *Where Do We Go from Here: Chaos or Community?*[7] There is no need to seek out rare archival materials to discern Dr. King's message; his speeches and writings are crystal clear. In this time of acute national malaise, his words have much to offer us as a prescription for the way forward.

1

⚛

What We Remember

M artin Luther King Jr. was born into an exceptional family in Atlanta, Georgia, in 1929. His father, a Morehouse graduate, was a
Baptist minister and civil rights leader active in the NAACP. His mother,
Alberta Williams, was a graduate of Hampton University, where she
trained as a teacher, although her teaching career was cut short by laws
that precluded married women from teaching. Both of Dr. King's parents
had a long history with the Ebenezer Baptist Church. Alberta's father
(Dr. King's maternal grandfather) was the minister there at the time that
she married King Sr., who after the death of Alberta's father in 1931 became
Ebenezer's minister, serving in this capacity for four decades.

Both of Dr. King's parents were active in their community and in the
fight to end segregation. Martin Luther King Sr. had an enormous influence on his son and on his "maladjustment" (as he would later call it)
to a system that disenfranchised, marginalized, and humiliated African
Americans.[1] Dr. King's father made certain that young Martin appreciated
the challenges faced by those less fortunate; he often sent him to work in
the fields to experience firsthand the kind of hard life that was the lot of
so many.

From an early age, King was an exceptional student. At the age of
fifteen, after skipping a couple of grades in his Atlanta high school, he
followed in his father's footsteps, enrolling at Morehouse College. He
graduated in 1948 with a degree in sociology. In 1951, he earned another
BA—this time in divinity—from Crozer Theological Seminary in Penn-

sylvania. In June 1955, just four years after completing his second BA, King received his PhD from the Boston University School of Theology. From his early years as the son of a minister to his advanced studies, Dr. King had a strong grounding in his faith. He was exceptionally well versed in Christian theology and the ethical precepts that he understood to be at the core of his religion and of all major world religions. Throughout all of his work, Dr. King drew inspiration from this faith and its emphasis on justice and compassion.

In 1953, Martin Luther King Jr. married Coretta Scott, an accomplished musician and activist. Coretta Scott had been one of the first black students to attend Antioch College, where she became active in the NAACP. She later transferred to the New England Conservatory of Music in Boston, where she graduated in 1954. It was during her time there that she met Martin, who was studying at Boston University. An exceptional woman who was fully committed to civil rights, she saw the civil rights movement as part of a larger campaign to liberate people worldwide from the bonds of poverty, violence, and discrimination. Ahead of her time on a woman's role in marriage, she took the rather unusual step of removing from her wedding vows the passage promising obedience to her husband. In the fall of 1954, a little more than a year after their marriage, the couple moved to Montgomery, Alabama, where Dr. King became the pastor of the Dexter Avenue Baptist Church.

In the years that followed, Dr. King took on the leadership of the Montgomery Improvement Association and the bus boycott triggered in December 1955 by Rosa Parks's refusal to give up her seat on a public bus (but actually set in motion long before that by committed activists in the NAACP and other groups). This year-long boycott led to the Supreme Court ruling in November 1956 that segregation of city buses was unconstitutional.

In 1963, Dr. King led the Birmingham Campaign, a prolonged campaign of resistance against widespread racial discrimination. It is most poignantly remembered in images of police aiming high-powered fire hoses at children—images that shocked the nation and the world. It was there that King was jailed and wrote his famous "Letter from Birmingham City Jail." Later, in *Why We Can't Wait*, he wrote of Birmingham that the "ultimate tragedy... was not the brutality of the bad people, but the silence of the good people."[2] This was a theme he would return to again and again.

Later that year, in August 1963, Washington, D.C., was the site of the March for Jobs and Freedom, which drew some 200,000 to 300,000 people—most of them African Americans—and where Dr. King delivered his "I Have a Dream" speech, parts of which form the core of our collective memory of Martin Luther King Jr.

In October 1964, Martin Luther King Jr. was awarded the prestigious Nobel Peace Prize.[3] He was just thirty-five years old at the time, the youngest person to have ever received the Nobel Prize. This was a turning point and reflected his stature as an international figure to be reckoned with. In accepting the prize, he renewed his commitment to nonviolence, all the while acknowledging the extreme levels of violence to which civil rights demonstrators were being subjected and which continued to be the lot of African Americans throughout the nation.

In 1965, he worked with the Southern Christian Leadership Council and other groups to organize the Selma to Montgomery marches for voting rights. Images from these marches—of police charging protestors with billy clubs, firing teargas, and brutally attacking peaceful demonstrators—were televised around the world.

August 1965 saw the Los Angeles neighborhood of Watts go up in flames in a massive rebellion triggered, as were the 1992 uprisings some thirty years later, by police brutality directed at African Americans, and more generally by overcrowding, economic depression, and other expressions of societal racism. This was not the first, nor was it the last, of many such urban rebellions that rocked the nation's cities over the next few years. Dr. King traveled to Watts, where he spoke about the conditions that led to the "riots" and urged that these be addressed through massive antipoverty programs to address the conditions in northern and western ghettos. This marked the move of the civil rights movement out of the South, where it had focused on challenging laws, to the rest of the country, where it focused on the economic consequences of racism. This is precisely where our memory of Dr. King grows weak.

In 1966, Dr. King moved his family north to Chicago, where he worked with others in the Chicago Freedom Movement. His civil rights concerns now emphasized economic equality; he could see that the legal gains of the civil rights movement had had no effect in alleviating the grinding poverty of the northern ghettos. He noted that in the Lawndale neighborhood of Chicago, the African American neighborhood where he settled, rents were higher than for modern apartments in the suburbs—and this for smaller apartments with fewer amenities. Yet, restrictive covenants forced African Americans into overcrowded, dilapidated areas of the city.

At the same time that Dr. King was turning his attention to the economic issues facing African Americans outside the South, our involvement in Vietnam was escalating. Over the next two years, Dr. King spoke out forcefully against economic inequality in the United States and worked closely with labor unions in opposing the war in Vietnam. His 1967 address at the Riverside Church in New York was a clear indictment of what he saw as a highly unjust war and misuse of national resources at a time when they were desperately needed to correct widespread poverty at home.

On April 1968, Dr. King was assassinated in Memphis, Tennessee, where he had gone to support striking sanitation workers. Joining with organized labor to support poor, black workers was controversial, and Dr. King was, as he had been for some time, under heavy government surveillance. He had become unpopular with the administration due to his outspoken opposition to the war in Vietnam, his support of labor, and his central role in the Poor People's Campaign, which was planning a massive, multiracial march on Washington. The official version that he was assassinated by James Earl Ray was called into question by the 1999 wrongful death case filed by the King family. In this civil case, which received little notice by the media, a jury of six black and six white jurors found that the assassination of Dr. King was carried out by a conspiracy involving the U.S. government, as alleged by Loyd Jowers in 1993, and that James Earl Ray was a scapegoat. The full transcript of the trial is available in the archives of the King Center.[4]

DR. KING AND THE CIVIL RIGHTS MOVEMENT

> In winning rights for ourselves we have produced substantial benefits for the whole nation.
> Martin Luther King Jr., *Where Do We Go from Here?*

Dr. King is now best remembered as a leader of the civil rights movement in the United States, a movement that challenged racist laws that barred

African Americans from full participation in civic and political life. We tend to forget that Dr. King was a very controversial figure whose tactics—nonviolent as they were—were nevertheless rejected as too radical by many African Americans as well as whites. Now, some fifty years later, it may be hard to imagine a world where black and white were legally required to drink from different drinking fountains and where the full force of the law came down on those who dared challenge such laws, but this was the situation in the southern United States of the 1950s, at the outset of Dr. King's involvement in the movement. It is a tribute to the commitment, fearlessness, and hope of all those involved that the Civil Rights movement was able, against enormous odds, to effectively dismantle legal segregation and the laws that excluded African Americans from all sorts of public goods—restaurants, hotels, recreational facilities such as parks and swimming pools, transportation, and importantly, the ballot box.

At the end of 1955, King was named as the head of the Montgomery Improvement Association. It was in his capacity as leader of the Montgomery bus boycott that he captured the public's attention and put the civil rights movement on the map. It was at this early stage of his work that Dr. King became an advocate of nonviolence, a philosophy and practice that would guide his life and work.

In the spring of 1963, in his position as the first president of the Southern Christian Leadership Conference, King joined with Fred Shuttlesworth of the Alabama Christian Movement for Human Rights to launch the Birmingham Campaign. This was a massive and sustained series of nonviolent direct actions aimed at dismantling the laws and customs that had made Birmingham the most segregated city in the South. Dr. King insisted that the campaign follow the precepts of nonviolence and gave a number of talks and training sessions on the practice of nonviolence. The use of nonviolent action was met with violent response from the city's leadership, notably the police chief "Bull" O'Connor, whose officers unleashed dogs and high-power water hoses on protesters, including the high school and even younger students who were part of the campaign.

More than any prior event, the Birmingham Campaign brought to national and international attention the brutal reality of the Jim Crow South. (Jim Crow refers to state and local laws enacted between 1876 and 1965 that mandated racial segregation in all public facilities—schools, transportation, restaurants and hotels, libraries, public pools, and even drinking fountains.) There were boycotts of local businesses, sit-ins at libraries and lunch counters, voter registration drives, and other peaceful protests. When an injunction outlawing the protests passed, huge numbers of people were arrested, overwhelming the capacity of local jails. Dr. King was among those arrested; it was there that he penned his famous "Letter from Birmingham Jail."[5] Labor unions, which continued to support King in the years following, provided important support in raising bail funds. The Birmingham Campaign also engaged the Kennedy administration, which sent federal troops to the city. In June of that year, President John F. Kennedy delivered a civil rights address to the nation, an address that was certainly triggered by the events in Alabama. In it, Kennedy spoke in support of immediate desegregation of all facilities open to the public and of enhanced voter protections. Importantly, he also made a point of noting that racial injustice was an issue across the United States and not just in the South and urged all Americans to join the struggle for equal rights for African Americans.[6]

Dr. King could see, however, that success of the civil rights movement in eliminating racist laws did not necessarily lead to racial equality. He was clear that, beginning with the Emancipation Proclamation in 1863, legislation to protect the rights of African Americans had been passed with no eye to implementation. In *Where Do We Go from Here: Chaos or Community?*, the book King wrote in 1967, a year before his death, he described the period of 1956 to 1966 as "the first phase." For most white Americans, this phase "had been a struggle to treat the Negro with a degree of decency, not of equality. White America," he went on to say, "was ready to demand that the Negro should be spared the lash of brutality and coarse degradation, but it had never been truly committed to helping him out of poverty, exploitation or all forms of discrimination."[7]

The civil rights movement triggered many changes in the legal structure of the United States:

- In 1956, following the Montgomery bus boycott, the Supreme Court ruled segregation on buses unconstitutional.
- In 1957, Congress passed the Civil Rights Act of 1957, the first civil rights legislation since Reconstruction. This was a voting rights act, ruling against poll taxes, literacy tests, and other local laws

designed to exclude African Americans from voting. (In 1957, only about 20 percent of African Americans were registered to vote; fifty years later that figure was around 68 percent.)

· The 1960 Civil Rights Act increased the capacity to implement and enforce the 1957 act. Both the 1957 and the 1960 Civil Rights Acts were passed under the Eisenhower administration.

· In 1961, President Kennedy signed Executive Order 10925, which prohibited discrimination in government hiring and established the President's Committee on Equal Employment Opportunity. This was later followed in 1965 by Executive Order 11246, signed into law by President Lyndon B. Johnson. These two executive orders established affirmative action as a way of ensuring equal opportunity in government employment.

· The 1964 Civil Rights Act, signed into law by President Johnson, outlawed discrimination in the workplace, in schools, and public accommodations (facilities serving the general public such as theaters, hotels, and restaurants) and led to the establishment in 1965 of the Equal Employment Opportunity Commission to enforce employment law. It also further strengthened voting rights by providing that rules and regulations governing voting be applied equally to all citizens.

· The 1965 Voting Rights Act, also signed by President Johnson, outlawed discriminatory practices such as literacy tests that were being used to keep African Americans from voting and established federal oversight of elections administration.

· In addition to these critical pieces of legislation, the civil rights movement, under Dr. King's leadership, was instrumental in advancing President Johnson's War on Poverty, which, although short-lived, did make significant differences in the nation. The overall poverty rate in the United States dropped from over 17 percent in 1964 to just over 11 percent in 1973, much of that attributable to the programs introduced by the War on Poverty.

· The Economic Opportunity Act of 1964 established the Office of Economic Opportunity which introduced programs such as Head Start, Job Corps, VISTA, food stamps, and the Community Action Program.

- The 1965 amendments to Social Security created Medicare and Medicaid.
- The Higher Education Act of 1965 established the Upward Bound program, which made college education a reality for many who had been excluded.
- The Civil Rights Act of 1968, passed in the wake of Dr. King's assassination, and also known as the Fair Housing Act, prohibited discrimination in housing.

These various pieces of legislation and the numerous safety net programs and legal protections for African Americans that they introduced made a real difference in terms of lowering the overall poverty rate and have protected millions of Americans from destitution. These are some of the formidable gains that can be attributed to the civil rights movement; unfortunately, they are now, and for several decades have been, under attack.

DR. KING AND NONVIOLENCE

> True nonviolence is more than the absence of violence. It is the persistent and determined application of peaceable power to offenses against the community.
>   Martin Luther King Jr., *Where Do We Go from Here?*

Along with his leadership role in the civil rights movement, Martin Luther King Jr. is remembered throughout the world for his advocacy and practice of nonviolence. Dr. King was committed to "militant, powerful, massive, nonviolence"[8] as a tool for social change. While the philosophy of nonviolence and civil disobedience surely pre-dates Dr. King, he became the face of nonviolent protest in the United States and throughout the world.

Dr. King showed the world that nonviolent approaches can and do work. Through nonviolent protest, the civil rights movement was able to strike down laws enforcing legal segregation. For King, nonviolence was a moral challenge; its objective was to call attention to injustice. But, he warned, nonviolence is not for the weak of heart. He saw nonviolence as a powerful demand for justice, to be backed up by massive organizing, pressure, and the "coercive power" of collective action such as boycotts. But, he noted, "If it [nonviolent action] is rudely rebuked, it is not transformed into resignation and passivity."[9] In this respect he reminded us that there are limits to patience and that Black Power and violent urban rebellions, which were often pointed to as justification for white resistance, were more likely a direct consequence of white resistance to the changes being demanded through nonviolent action.

It may come as a surprise to learn that Dr. King, while a believer in nonviolence and someone who had studied it extensively, was not always a practitioner of nonviolence. Dr. King was a great admirer of Mahatma Gandhi. Known for his courage and discipline in using nonviolent tactics to confront the injustices of British rule in his homeland of India, Gandhi had developed his theory and practice of nonviolence while living in South Africa as a young lawyer. After he returned to India, he became the leader of the Indian National Congress and is best remembered for his pivotal role in the nonviolent Quit India movement that finally led to India's independence from Great Britain. Martin Luther King drew inspiration from Gandhi's work and even made a pilgrimage to his birthplace in what is now Gujarat, India.

However, it was the influence of a lesser-known but pivotal figure in the civil rights movement that led Dr. King and his colleagues to actually adopt the practice of nonviolence. Bayard Rustin, an African American raised in the Quaker tradition, was deeply committed to the Quaker value of nonviolence. He served prison time as a conscientious objector in World War II, and had worked with Gandhi's nonviolent Quit India movement. Rustin was on the front lines in fighting injustice. He worked with the American Friends Service Committee to defend the rights of Japanese Americans who had been placed in detention centers during the war, was part of the South African antiapartheid movement, and had spent extended periods in Africa working with Kwame Nkrumah in Ghana and Nnamdi Azikiwe in Nigeria. King's senior by many years (he was born in 1912), Rustin was a lifelong pacifist and advocate for the rights of marginalized groups, and was also unapologetically gay in a time when that was a distinct liability. It was Rustin who schooled King and his colleagues in the actual practice of nonviolence and its critical place in the civil rights movement. A brilliant strategist, an exceptional organizer, and a stalwart advocate of nonviolence, Bayard Rustin was a major influence on King and on the entire civil rights movement.

Rustin joined Dr. King shortly after he was named head of the Montgomery Improvement Association. He had been urged to do so by his friend Lillian Smith, the outspoken critic of racism and author (*Strange Fruit*, 1944; *Killers of the Dream*, 1949), who asked that he go to Montgomery to advise King and his colleagues in the use of nonviolence. Upon his arrival there, Rustin found that members of the association were armed. As targets of violent threats, they understandably felt the need to protect themselves. Rustin was able not only to convince them to get rid of their guns, but to make nonviolence the central core of all their work. Rustin remained a key figure in the civil rights movement, serving as organizer and advisor. It was Rustin who was the major strategist and organizer for various campaigns and events, not the least of which was the 1963 March on Washington. It was through his association with Rustin that Dr. King's nonviolence went from theoretical to practical and he came to adopt the practice of nonviolence as the key strategy of the civil rights movement.

Dr. King's adherence to nonviolence was both philosophical and practical. It was philosophical in that he believed that nonviolent resistance to unjust laws is a moral obligation, not one of several moral options, that one has a moral responsibility to disobey unjust laws. "We must never forget," he said, "that everything Adolf Hitler did in Germany was 'legal.'"[10] Passive cooperation with an unjust system, failure to resist immoral laws, makes the oppressed as evil as their oppressors.

Moreover, he insisted that nonviolent civil disobedience must be done "openly, lovingly, and with a willingness to accept the penalty."[11] For Dr. King, nonviolent civil disobedience was a deeply spiritual practice and required serious preparation and purification of intent to remove anger and selfishness.[12] In his "Letter from Birmingham Jail," Dr. King explained the purpose of nonviolent protest:

> Nonviolent direct action seeks to create such a crisis and foster such a tension that a community which has constantly refused to negotiate is forced to confront the issue. It seeks to so dramatize the issue that it can no longer be ignored. My citing the creation of tension as part of the work of the nonviolent-resister may sound rather shocking. But I must confess that I am not afraid of the word "tension." I have earnestly opposed violent

tension, but there is a type of constructive, nonviolent tension which is necessary for growth.

In the movement for civil rights, Dr. King was keenly aware that violence was not a practical strategy for success; the odds were so obviously uneven. "Anyone leading a violent rebellion," Dr. King wrote, "must be willing to make an honest assessment regarding the possible casualties to a minority population confronting a well-armed, wealthy majority with a fanatical right wing that would delight in exterminating thousands of black men, women and children."[13] In addition to its being impractical, King noted that violence drew attention away from the issues, becoming itself the focus of attention.

Largely thanks to Dr. King's work, nonviolence has become a standard tool for social change, and training in nonviolence is a regular part of many social protest movements around the world. King's influence in putting nonviolence on the map, particularly in the United States, cannot be overstated. We have seen nonviolence take on worldwide importance in countless social justice campaigns. The Occupy Wall Street movement, for example, was grounded in the principles of nonviolence. Occupy began in September 2011 in New York City and had within a month spread to eighty-two countries around the world, becoming a global protest against militarism, greed, and racism—the very cornerstones of Martin Luther King Jr.'s thinking.

2

What We Forget: Dr. King's Warnings
about the "Giant Triplets"

D r. King was a great leader of the civil rights movement; he lived,
practiced, and made popular the principles of nonviolent protest.
But he did so much more that our collective memories leave out of the
picture. Martin Luther King Jr. was not only an activist and public figure;
he was one of the great thinkers of the twentieth century. From the very
beginning of his public life, Dr. King spoke and wrote about three forces,
militarism, materialism, and racism, which he saw as serious moral threats
to our country and our world. He called these the Giant Triplets: "giant" because of their huge corrosive power; "triplets" because their "lives"
are so closely intertwined that it is difficult to disentangle them. He was
a critic of the increasing militarism of the United States and urged the
country to aggressively pursue peace and put an end to war as a means of
resolving conflict, he spoke out for economic justice and was an advocate
of a guaranteed minimum living wage. And he was a strong advocate of
reparations as a path to achieving racial justice. He spoke about deep-
seated institutional issues that demanded institutional solutions, which
in turn demanded the will of the public to achieve them. He talked about
changing the structure of U.S. society and government to enact policies
to promote peace rather than war, to assure a degree of economic fairness,
and to address racism and its legacies.

These themes were already clear in one of his earlier speeches in September 1957, delivered on the occasion of the twenty-fifth anniversary of

the Highlander Folk School, a training center in rural Tennessee for labor organizers and civil rights leaders:

> There are some things in our social system to which I am proud to be maladjusted and to which I suggest that you, too, ought to be maladjusted. I never intend to adjust myself to the viciousness of mob rule. I never intend to adjust myself to the evils of segregation and the crippling effects of discrimination. I never intend to adjust myself to the tragic inequalities of an economic system which takes necessities from the masses to give luxuries to the classes. I never intend to become adjusted to the madness of militarism and the self-defeating method of physical violence.[1]

Combating militarism, materialism, and racism was at the core of what Dr. King stood for. His leadership of the civil rights movement and his advocacy of nonviolence must be seen as part of the larger struggle against these three evils.

Listening today to the most famous lines from the "I Have a Dream" speech, we Americans are deeply moved, seeing how far we have come—with the election of a black president, no less. But in fact we have all but ignored the issues about which Dr. King spoke out most forcefully. We have stepped backward in many respects, becoming a more warlike society, and one with growing extremes of social inequality. If someone devotes his life to planting trees, it's disingenuous to claim to honor his memory while bulldozing the forest. Yet it sometimes seems that that is just what we are doing to Dr. King's legacy.

MILITARISM

> It is as possible and as urgent to put an end to war and violence between nations as it is to put an end to poverty and racial injustice.
>   Martin Luther King Jr., *Where Do We Go from Here?*

Militarism, "the tendency to regard military efficiency as the supreme ideal of the state and to subordinate all other interests to those of the military,"[2] is grounded in the belief that violence is an effective means of resolving conflict. Military approaches to conflict contrast with those that focus on negotiation, empathy and perspective taking, and willingness to compromise.

Dr. King was convinced that the fight for racial justice and economic equality would be futile if nations continued in their warlike behaviors. He was criticized for speaking out against U.S. militarism and, in particular, against the war in Vietnam. He was tracked by the FBI, castigated by the media, and threatened for "stepping out of his place" as a civil rights leader. But for Dr. King, the fight against militarism and the fight for civil rights were part of the same struggle; both were about justice. To separate them would be, as he put it, "to segregate my moral concerns."[3] He believed that there can be no justice without peace, and no peace without justice.

Even though Dr. King was one of the most outspoken critics of our military involvement in Vietnam and elsewhere, his name is seldom invoked in the context of the antiwar/peace movement of the 1960s. It is worth asking why this should be the case, and why his antiwar message is no longer part of popular memory. Dr. King is so firmly associated with civil rights that other aspects of his message have faded into obscurity. In truth, African Americans are rarely associated with the antiwar movement, perhaps because the analysis they offered of our involvement and its racist underpinnings raises larger issues about our national character that we have not been willing to face. The prizefighter Muhammad Ali, who was an outspoken critic of U.S. military adventures, is more likely to be associated with the politics of Black Power than with the antiwar movement. Bayard Rustin, a committed pacifist and a leading strategist in the civil rights movement, had been a conscientious objector during World War II and was certainly one of the most important antiwar activists of the twentieth century. But few even recognize his name. Rustin, too, was an African American. We seem to have forgotten that there was significant African American resistance to the draft (the "all-volunteer army" had not yet come into being) and to the war itself, especially among the Nation of Islam.

Perhaps not unrelated to this reluctance to recognize African American voices in the peace movement is the pervasive belief that Dr. King developed his critique of militarism late in his public life and only in response to escalating U.S. military engagement in Vietnam. That is simply not true: Dr. King's position on militarism was already quite clear in his 1957 address at the Highlander Folk School when he said, "I never intend to become adjusted to the madness of militarism and the self-defeating method of physical violence."[4] From the beginning of his public life, Dr. King was an outspoken critic of using violence to force an enemy into submission—whether perpetrated by individuals or by nations through their militaries. In a 1957 address at the Dexter Avenue Baptist Church, he spoke of how "force begets force, hate begets hate, and toughness begets toughness."[5]

In 1959, in response to criticisms that he was inconsistent in opposing the violence of war, Dr. King stated clearly his antiwar stance: "Merely to set the record straight, may I state that repeatedly, in public addresses and in my writings, I have unequivocally declared my hatred for this most colossal of all evils and I have condemned any organizer of war, regardless of his rank or nationality. I have signed numerous statements with other Americans condemning nuclear testing and have authorized publication of my name in advertisements appearing in the largest circulation news-papers in the country, without concern that it was then 'unpopular' to so speak out."[6]

When Dr. King was awarded the Nobel Peace Prize in 1964, the *New York Times* reminded readers that the purpose of the prize was to honor acts "for the furtherance of brotherhood among men and to the abolishment or reduction of standing armies and for the extension of these purposes."[7] In his acceptance speech, Dr. King stated, "I refuse to accept the cynical notion that nation after nation must spiral down a militaristic stairway into the hell of thermonuclear destruction. . . . I believe that even amid today's mortar bursts and whining bullets, there is still hope for a brighter tomorrow. . . . I have the audacity to believe that peoples everywhere can have three meals a day for their bodies, education and culture for their minds, and dignity, equality and freedom for their spirits."[8]

If Dr. King became a more outspoken critic of the military in the last few years of his life, it is because our military engagement in Vietnam required that he do so. He was widely criticized for his antiwar activism. White America and the powers that be could accept him as a spokesperson for the civil rights movement, but not when he spoke out forcefully about our military engagements. He was told that civil rights and peace don't mix. His outspoken denunciation of our involvement in Vietnam cost him many former allies. But Dr. King's opposition to the war in Vietnam

followed from larger concerns about militarism and racism and his commitment to the philosophy and practice of nonviolence. In his famous
Riverside Church address of April 1967, he reminded his audience that,
as the recipient of the Nobel Peace Prize, he had a responsibility and an
obligation "to work harder than I had ever worked before for 'the brotherhood of man.'"[9]

Dr. King spoke about the nonviolence he continued to preach at home
among angry youth, and how that was at odds with the escalating violence
of war overseas.

> As I have walked among the desperate, rejected, and angry young men,
> I have told them that Molotov cocktails and rifles would not solve their
> problems. I have tried to offer them my deepest compassion while
> maintaining my conviction that social change comes most meaningfully
> through nonviolent action. But they asked, and rightly so, "What about
> Vietnam?" They asked if our own nation wasn't using massive doses of
> violence to solve its problems, to bring about the changes it wanted. Their
> questions hit home, and I knew that I could never again raise my voice
> against the violence of the oppressed in the ghettos without having first
> spoken clearly to the greatest purveyor of violence in the world today: my
> own government. For the sake of those boys, for the sake of this govern-
> ment, for the sake of the hundreds of thousands trembling under our
> violence, I cannot be silent.[10]

He questioned the moral grounds of military engagements that he saw
as being in the service of imperialism and neocolonialism and that served
the rich and were paid for with the lives of the poor. Dr. King spoke out
against the human costs of war and the fact that investment in military
solutions meant disinvestment in much-needed social goods. Moreover,
he was convinced that military "solutions" to conflict were not solutions
at all; not only were they ineffectual, but they fueled conflict rather than
resolving it.

Dr. King called for the powerful pursuit of peace through nonviolence
and an end to what he called "talking peace while preparing for war."[11]
Peace, he wrote, "is not merely a distant goal that we seek but a *means*
by which we arrive at that goal" (my emphasis).[12] This is a key piece of
his thinking: peace is not only the end to be sought, but the means by
which to get there. Peace cannot be successfully pursued through mili-

tary avenues—waging war to attain peace, he contended, simply will not work. While he allowed that in the past war may have served to prevent the growth and spread of evil forces, the increasing sophistication and destructive power of modern weaponry "eliminates even the possibility that war may serve any good at all. If we assume that life is worth living and that man has a right to survive," he went on, "then we must find an alternative to war."[13]

Nonviolence requires the aggressive and creative pursuit of peace. The peace offensive Dr. King called for requires determination and courage. It requires dedication to resolving conflicts through negotiation and other peaceful means and an enduring commitment to rejecting violence as an option. It requires seeing one's enemies first and foremost as people. But it is a matter not just of ending war, but of affirming and pursuing peace. Dr. King emphasized over and over again the need for a change in focus, "a mental and spiritual re-evaluation,"[14] the shift from an arms race to a peace race. He urged that the philosophy and strategy of nonviolence become serious subjects for study and experimentation in all areas of human conflict, including conflicts among nations. In this respect, we have definitely acted upon Dr. King's recommendation. There are now numerous institutes for promoting peace and hundreds of colleges and universities across the country with excellent programs in peace and conflict studies, peace and justice, and peace and reconciliation. Each year, thousands of students follow these courses, and there is a clear interest in building peace. However, these programs have not translated into what Dr. King was talking about: government policies clearly aimed at the vigorous pursuit of peace. We are more heavily involved militarily than ever before. It is worth asking why these many initiatives have not been able to override the prevailing preference for military solutions.

In Washington for the inauguration of President Obama in his second term, former President Jimmy Carter said that he had tried to think of places where the United States has promoted peace. He could not think of one. He asked John Kerry, at the time just appointed as secretary of state, whether he could think of anywhere on earth that the United States is now trying to promote peace. Kerry's answer was "No." President Carter noted that since 1979, "the United States has constantly been at war, and I would say that the most critical aspect of other people looking at the United

States has been that we are warlike, we tend to resolve every dispute by going to war. We are now threatening to go into Mali, we are threatening to go into Iran, and so forth."[15]

Carter went on to say, as regards the U.S. record on human rights:

> The United States was in the forefront of developing the Universal Declaration of Human Rights at the end of the Second World War. Eleanor Roosevelt, the widow of Franklin D. Roosevelt, went there and declared the Universal Declaration of Human Rights. There are 30 paragraphs in the declaration. The United States at this moment is violating 10 of the 30 paragraphs. We now are detaining people in prison, without a trial and without an accusation presented against them, for life. Half the people in Guantánamo Bay, in the prison there, have never been tried and have never been accused of a crime, but will be in prison for the rest of their lives. And the United States is now using drones, as you know, to go into foreign countries with which we are not at war, and committing executions.[16]

After 9/11 and the terrible events that left nearly three thousand people dead, the United States had the opportunity to become a beacon for peace and to turn away from militarism and seek peaceful responses. This was not impossible. Here again, Dr. King's words have resonance: "We can no longer afford to worship the God of hate or bow down before the altar of retaliation."[17] Instead of using our moral power to spread a message of peace, we chose to up the ante, by launching the so-called War on Terror. As I write this in 2013, this "war" has been going on for over a decade and has entailed enormous and extremely costly militarization, not only of the United States, but of the entire world and has significantly reduced any reserves of goodwill we may have enjoyed. We spoke of peace, but responded with war. In 2013, the United States was once again rattling its sabers—this time at Iran—on grounds not unlike those used as the pretext for invading Iraq in 2003—an invasion that resulted in enormous destruction and human suffering.

Being the most powerful country in the world does not give us the right to force others to do our bidding; yet, judging from our expenditures, our preferred method of interacting with the rest of the world is through military force. The 2012 U.S. defense budget topped $700 billion, compared to a foreign aid budget in the neighborhood of $50 billion.[18] U.S. military spending dwarfs that of other nations, accounting for more than 40 percent of the world's military expenditures. In 2012, the U.S. military budget was six times greater than that of China and eleven times greater than Russia's.[19] This includes maintaining abroad more than a half million soldiers (each costing annually more than $500,000 to support), intelligence agents, technicians, teachers, dependents, and civilian contractors.[20] In spite of its demonstrated lack of effectiveness and high costs, we continue to invest our national fortunes in this approach to resolving conflict. It is of interest to look into who benefits from these huge public (i.e., taxpayer) investments in the military.

Militarism serves the interests of the few at the expense of the many. The "military-industrial complex" that President Dwight D. Eisenhower warned against in his farewell address[21]—weapons manufacturers, military suppliers, and the military itself—represents a dangerous conflation of public and private interests. This "partnership" increasingly includes private military/security companies like Blackwater USA (now Academi), which has been involved in numerous scandals involving arms smuggling and the murder of civilians. It also includes giant contracting companies like Halliburton (for which former vice president Dick Cheney—a major proponent of the War on Terror—served as chairman and CEO from 1995 to 2000) and its many subsidiaries. These firms make enormous profits from military contracts for building and maintaining military bases and military detention centers and providing other support to the military. The levels of corruption and waste in these undertakings are shocking.[22] These same firms are involved in the multibillion-dollar business of reconstruction—attempting to undo the damage of our military interventions. In a March 2013 radio interview, Stuart Bowen, the inspector general for Iraq reconstruction, said that the cost to U.S. taxpayers of Iraq reconstruction, which he deemed fraught with waste and fraud, was in the neighborhood of $60 billion. And for Afghanistan, he estimated the cost of reconstruction to be $90 billion.[23] The leadership of these private firms is so closely intertwined with those in high-level positions in the U.S. government that conflicts of interest between private gain and public good are unavoidable.

The human costs of our expanding military engagements fall to the many young soldiers killed or injured in combat and to the many more civilians who are caught in the cross fire or who become victims of the by-products of violent conflict—hunger, disease, displacement, and despair. Over an eleven-year period from October 2001 to August 2012, more than 6,500 American troops lost their lives and upward of 42,000 were wounded.[24] These were for the most part young people just beginning their adult lives. Among those who returned from military service in these wars, there was a high incidence of depression, mental illness, physical disability, and substance abuse. The suicide rate among both active service military and veterans became alarmingly high. Many, upon return to the United States, found themselves homeless. At this writing, almost one-quarter of the homeless in the United States are veterans, and more than half of all homeless veterans are African American or Hispanic, despite the fact that African Americans constitute just 17 percent of active duty forces[25] and only 10.3 percent of the veteran population.[26]

Until the shift from a draft to a volunteer army in 1973, the burden of our military engagements was at least theoretically shared equally by all (young male) Americans. Admittedly, even during the draft, the privileged found various ways, such as college deferments, to avoid service. Still, the specter of being called up for active duty meant that the value and morality of our military engagements were more closely scrutinized across social classes. I can still feel the visceral anxiety that accompanied each announcement: Would my brother be called? If so, would he go? Would he come back alive? And for what? Today, the fact that we are not uniformly confronted with the possibility of having our brothers and sisters, our spouses, our children, or ourselves conscripted into military service has made it easier for us to engage in what might otherwise be very unpopular wars. The low level of protest against the excesses of the current War on Terror may be partly due to the fact that the burden of fighting it is not equally distributed among the middle and upper classes. If it were, we would likely find antiwar protest levels not unlike those during the Vietnam War.

As we have lashed out, seeking to find and punish those responsible for 9/11, we have wreaked havoc in the countries where we have chosen to wage this War on Terror, leaving death and destruction in our wake. Conservative estimates put the number of Iraqi civilian deaths at over 110,000; other counts reach to over a million.[27] The U.S. invasion of Iraq and the subsequent occupation have completely destabilized the country, destroyed infrastructure, and introduced levels of violence that continue well after the official disengagement of U.S. forces. Estimates of civilian deaths in Afghanistan due to the U.S. invasion come to more than

13,000.[28] This does not include deaths in other countries such as Yemen, Somalia, and Pakistan, or the millions who have been wounded, lost family members, fled to other countries as refugees, or become internally displaced.

The United States has committed to pulling its combat troops out of Afghanistan by 2014. But as the War on Terror spreads into West Africa and the Sahara, we can expect more deaths, more disruption, and growing resentment from those who are caught in the crossfire.

Dr. King believed that the best defense against our enemies lies not in war, but rather in taking "offensive action in behalf of justice."[29] In reference to the war in Vietnam, he said, "There will be no meaningful solution [to war] until some attempt is made to know these people and to hear their broken cries."[30] This is not likely to be achieved by the targeted killings, civilian deaths, extrajudicial rendition, and systematic use of torture that have become standard operating procedures of the War on Terror. Dr. King rejected the rationale that virtually anything goes in the fight against communism. If we replace "communism" with "terrorism," we can see the continuing relevance of his message: "Nothing provides the Communists [terrorists] with a better climate for expansion and infiltration than the continued alliance of our nation with racism and exploitation throughout the world."[31] Our best defense, he noted, will be in our efforts to "remove those conditions of poverty, insecurity and injustice which are the fertile soil in which the seed of Communism [terrorism] grows and develops."[32] Instead, then and now, we have chosen to sow death and destruction through military approaches to problems that can really be solved only by a turn toward justice in our relations with the rest of the world.

Dr. King reminded us that violence of any sort, including violence justified by military logic, is an ineffective means of resolving disputes, is likely to escalate the conflict, and is the cause of much human suffering. "Time is cluttered," Dr. King reminds us, "with the wreckage of individuals and communities that surrendered to hatred and violence."[33]

Diversion of Resources

As someone who was intent on building the Beloved Community, a society where all are accorded basic dignity and respect, Dr. King was well aware that investments in the military translate as disinvestments in building peaceful communities—schools, housing, parks, job creation, and assurance that all members of society have a decent life. "A nation that continues year after year to spend more money on military defense than on programs of social uplift," he wrote, "is approaching spiritual death."[34] As President Dwight D. Eisenhower noted in April 1953, "every gun that is made, every warship launched, every rocket fired signifies in the final sense, a theft from those who hunger and are not fed, those who are cold and are not clothed. This world in arms is not spending money alone. It is spending the sweat of its laborers, the genius of its scientists, the hopes of its children. This is not a way of life at all in any true sense. Under the clouds of war, it is humanity hanging on a cross of iron."[35]

Like President Eisenhower before him, Dr. King had done the math: money spent on wars is money not spent on social goods. In a 1967 speech to the National Labor Leadership Assembly for Peace, Dr. King noted that Congress was voting an annual $35 billion for war and not even $2 billion for the War on Poverty.[36] In 2012, the war budget topped $700 billion, while the War on Poverty was only a fading memory.

National security has become a frequent topic of conversation, if not a national obsession. These discussions almost always take as a given that national security is primarily about external threats. But there are internal threats, as well, that can eat away at our security as a nation. Ours is a nation where between 1.5 and 3.5 million (when factoring in those who do not seek shelter) people are homeless[37] and 2.3 million people incarcerated,[38] with 6 million under correctional supervision[39] (an inordinate number of whom are African Americans). More than 45 million Americans have no health insurance,[40] and more than 50 million Americans live in food-insecure households.[41] Millions of people have lost their homes to foreclosure. Our lack of preparedness for natural disasters like Katrina and Sandy has left tens of thousands of people (again, an inordinate number of whom are poor and African Americans) without homes. Given these conditions, we would do well to rethink the idea of national security.

Nor should we ignore the very real problem of crumbling infrastructure: roads, bridges, water systems, and electricity grids are everywhere falling into disrepair, which leaves us open to further disasters. At the same time, mass shootings here at home have introduced a new element of danger to everyday life. In 2012, a mass shooting at an elementary school in the sleepy white suburb of Newtown, Connecticut, took the lives of twenty-eight people (mostly children). There were thirteen such incidents in that year alone.[42] We can no longer assume we are safe and secure—at school, at the shopping center, at the movies, or at our places of work. If the definition of terrorism is that which instills terror, then these mass shootings certainly fit the definition. The people who lived in the largely African American neighborhood of the lower Ninth Ward of New Orleans during the flooding that followed in the aftermath of Hurricane Katrina know something about terror, as well—as much from the contemptuous response to their suffering as from the destruction of the hurricane itself. In short, there are many internal threats to our security. We are taken by surprise when they hit, but we should not be; we invest very few serious resources in guarding against them—largely because we are so distracted by chasing (and, in the process, actually creating) foreign demons. We would do well to take note of historian Arnold Toynbee's observation, cited by Dr. King, that the decline and fall of almost all major world civilizations was caused not by external invasion but by internal decay.[43]

Widespread poverty, fear of arrest and imprisonment, fear of losing one's job and home, and increasing gun violence—these are very real threats for growing numbers of Americans. Can we really feel secure under these circumstances? It is worth seriously reconsidering the meaning of national security. Can a country be considered secure when one in six of its people does not have enough to eat and a significant portion of its population is living in despair and fear? When the levels of social inequality have reached such extremes? A problem with seeking security through growing militarism is that it invests an inordinate portion of tax revenue into guarding against just one threat to security while neglecting to protect against other, at least equally dangerous, threats.

Martin Luther King Jr.'s Riverside Church sermon of April 4, 1967, in which he denounced U.S. involvement in Vietnam, is often cited as the beginning of his outspoken opposition to the Vietnam War. In fact, Dr. King's opposition had been growing over the years as the war escalated and the gains of the civil rights movement failed to be followed by any action. The vast majority of African Americans were still living in cities characterized by "decay, squalor, and pollution"[44] across the country. The irony was not lost on Dr. King. He saw the spectacle of the United States investing billions of dollars to wage war in a far-off corner of the world on a people who were not an immediate threat, while at home huge numbers of people were living in poverty. For Dr. King, our involvement in Vietnam was immoral and unjust and a shameful misuse of public resources. "Why," he asked, "has our nation placed itself in the position of being God's military agent on earth? . . . Why have we substituted the arrogant undertaking of policing the world for the high task of putting our own house in order?"[45] We might ask ourselves the same questions today. We continue to invest larger and larger sums of money into policing the world, and our own house is still in disorder on a growing number of counts.

The United States is the number-one arms exporter in the world, a position it has held for some time.[46] Our arsenal of high-tech weaponry has grown increasingly sophisticated. It now includes, for example, the costly and controversial drone, a remotely controlled aircraft capable of attacking targets thousands of miles away. Drones come in a number of models, each with a price tag in the millions of dollars. Because drones are piloted remotely, often from base stations in the United States, the cost of establishing and maintaining base stations, equipment, and personnel must also be factored in. The 2012 budget request for the MQ-1 Predator and MQ-9 Reaper (now superseded by the Avenger—the name says it all), was well over $2.5 billion, slightly down from the 2011 allocation of just over $2.7 billion.[47] More disturbing than a drone's price is its function, which is, to quote General T. M. Moseley, former chief of staff of the U.S. Air Force, "a hunter-killer role." We are assured that these attacks are carefully targeted assassinations—itself morally problematic—but there have also been hundreds of civilian deaths associated with drone attacks. The precise number is unknown, but low estimates would certainly put the number at well over one thousand civilians, most of them in Pakistan. Drone strikes there increased significantly during the Obama administration.[48] As the War on Terror fans out into Africa with the establishment of a drone base in the West African country of Niger, it risks transforming the African continent into yet another military theater for our War on Terror.

Given its role as the world's biggest arms exporter, the United States has contributed significantly to littering the planet with arms, thereby increasing the deadly nature of conflicts. The weapons industry, an integral part of the militarist approach to managing conflict, is concerned with selling arms and not with where they end up. Land mines, which remain long after conflicts have subsided, not only have caused enormous civilian casualties, but continue as well to rob people of access to arable land and thus to food. U.S.-manufactured arms were among those from the Libyan conflict that made their way into the hands of extremists in northern Mali, facilitating their takeover of the north. While the United States provided military support that helped solve the immediate problem of rooting out the extremists, this operation also increased the stockpile of arms in the region. And even though the drone base in Niger is intended for intelligence purposes only, events in the region could prove it to be another slippery slope.

Our huge infusions of military aid to Israel continue to fuel violent conflict in the region and, in particular, Israel's destruction of Palestine and Palestinians. U.S. taxpayers pay a significant portion of this bill—well over $3 billion in 2012—or about one-fifth of the entire Israeli military budget. Since 1949, the United States has provided Israel with $115 billion in aid, most of it military aid.[49] This is a staggering amount to be spending mostly on weaponry and is no way to promote peace of any kind. It is no secret that this money goes to support U.S. and Israeli arms manufacturers, with the United States being the number-one arms exporter in the world and Israel in the top ten. These weapons travel far and wide in the arms trade and fuel deadly conflicts around the globe.

Yet, for all these investments of people and money, it is not at all clear the world has become a safer place in recent decades—although that depends on who and where you are. There is much more high-tech weaponry, and significantly more arms circulating worldwide, as well as in cities and towns here in the United States. Given that our growing investments in violence/military solutions are not having the desired effect, perhaps it would be worth trying another approach. Dr. King urged us to question this increasing militarism, and to ask questions about our national character without being intimidated by fears of being unpatriotic. He reminded us of the "strong strain of dissent in the American tradition, even in time of war."[50] We need to rethink what national security means and to broaden our thinking to include the many very real internal threats to our security. Dr. King's questions about our role in the world are worthy of reflection today: Are we indeed trying to be God's military agent on earth? Is this an appropriate role for the United States, or any other nation-state? The lack of public engagement around these issues and the lethargy, cynicism, and disengagement from public discourse that we are witnessing are harmful to our democracy.

Dr. King called for a revolution in values and a turning away from war. "A true revolution of values," he wrote, "will lay hands on the world order and say of war: 'This way of settling differences in not just.' This business of burning human beings with napalm, of filling our nation's homes with orphans and widows, of injecting poisonous drugs of hate into the veins of peoples normally humane, of sending men home from dark and bloody battlefields physically handicapped and psychologically deranged cannot be reconciled with wisdom, justice and love."[51] Real peace, Dr. King reminded us, is not just an absence of tension, but the presence of justice.

MATERIALISM

> True compassion is more than flinging a coin to a beggar; it understands that an edifice which produces beggars needs restructuring.
> Martin Luther King Jr., *Where Do We Go from Here?*

Materialism and militarism are closely related; it is the quest for wealth and power that drives militarism. "Violence," Dr. King wrote, "has been the inseparable twin of materialism, the hallmark of its grandeur and its misery."[52] Materialism can be defined as a preoccupation with accumulation of material goods and comforts, often accompanied by a lack of interest in spiritual or community values, intellectual or cultural pursuits. Dr. King described the dangers of being more thing-oriented than people-oriented, more interested in the accumulation of material goods than in doing right by others and contributing to our communities. A society that condones—and sometimes even celebrates—accumulation by a smaller and smaller proportion of the population will need major restructuring if we are to replace the prevailing ethos of greed with one of compassion and put an end to the "production of beggars."

Dr. King observed that "the richer we have become materially, the poorer we have become morally and spiritually."[53] A gauge of moral and spiritual wealth is how we treat one another. That we allow such extremely unequal distribution of wealth and opportunity in our society is what Dr. King was talking about when he spoke of moral and spiritual poverty.

The "culture of poverty" was an idea that became popular in the 1960s as a way of explaining why some people are poor. Poverty, according to this theory, is a consequence of the behavior patterns of poor people. This theory has been discredited, but that has not prevented it from becoming lodged in the national psyche. Young people continue to absorb the idea that poor people are responsible for their plight. In a recent conversation with an otherwise intelligent and compassionate young teacher, I was struck by her claim that, among other things, "poor people don't have the value of saving." It seemed to have escaped her notice that they have nothing to save. I raise this because it points to a major blind spot in dealing with poverty. The culture-of-poverty framework leads us to look for the roots of poverty in the wrong places: among the poor. It deflects our attention from the culture that produces poverty by its policies and practices. What kind of a culture allows widespread poverty in one of the world's richest countries? What kind of underlying values characterize a society in which 22 percent of children live in poverty?[54] (This 2011 figure is for the United States; in many parts of the world the proportion is much higher.) The focus on the supposed moral shortcomings of the poor makes invisible the very real moral shortcomings of the larger society and keeps us from addressing the problem at its roots.

Dr. King's focus may have been on the United States, but he was well aware that the situation at home was part of a larger, predatory economic system that created glaring inequalities throughout the world. He noted the practice of corporations investing huge sums of money in Africa, Asia, and Latin America and extracting the profits with no thought to investing in the places and populations from which their wealth derived. In Africa, this pattern has persisted, and even escalated, since the 1960s when most countries reclaimed their independence.

In the 2012 election year there was much talk about the chimera of a "growing middle class" but virtually no mention of the legions that had joined the ranks of the poor who are struggling to feed and house their families. Nor, for that matter, was there much mention of the three million or so people who control 40 percent of the nation's wealth, or the fact that in 2011, 46 million people—nearly one in six Americans—had incomes below the official poverty line. This silence reflects a gradual change in public discourse that has evolved over the last several presidencies.

From 1973 to 2007, as the minimum wage fell 22 percent in real dollars, domestic corporate profits jumped more than 50 percent—bloating the gap between rich and poor.[55] The ultimate effect has been the shrinking of the middle class. "Middle class" or a "middle-class life" generally means a standard of living that includes at the least adequate food and shelter, access to quality health care, and educational and cultural resources. Sometimes, but not always, it includes a college education or some kind of professional or skilled work training. And while homeownership is sometimes included as a criterion, its relevancy to achieving middle-class status is questionable. Those who own homes generally pay less for housing and so may be able to have a "middle-class" lifestyle with a lower income than those who rent. Those who have some accumulated wealth may also be able to make it on lower incomes and still be middle class. Here it is important to note that income and wealth are not synonymous. It is the accumulation of wealth (usually built up over generations) that keeps some people afloat while lack of it keeps others rooted in poverty in spite of earning middle-class incomes. One personal disaster, such as a health crisis, can plunge a family into poverty if their income is their only safety net. As we will see in the next chapter, the historical exclusion of African Americans from opportunities to accumulate wealth is a major factor in current racial disparities.

The place where the middle class has been shrinking is at the edge, where people have only a small margin of error, where the loss of a job or an unexpected illness can mean inability to make rent or mortgage payments, loss of one's home, and a spiraling descent into poverty. Banks' promotion of subprime mortgage loans tapped right into that vulnerable edge: as many as six and a half million homes were lost to foreclosure in the five or six years following 2006,[56] pushing entire families into poverty. It is no secret that the impact of home loss due to subprime lending, like many of the other ills affecting our economy, fell disproportionately on African Americans.

As one strategy for assuring that everyone has the basics for a decent life, Dr. King advocated the adoption of a guaranteed annual minimum living income for all Americans. "There is nothing," Dr. King wrote, "ex-

cept shortsightedness to prevent us from guaranteeing an annual minimum—and livable—income for every American family."[57] The guaranteed annual income he proposed was to be a sum of money paid to all
citizens, regardless of income or employment status, to assure that each
is able to secure adequate housing, nutrition, health care, and education.
It would guarantee that everyone have the basics for a decent life without
stripping them of their autonomy in managing their resources.

Proponents of the guaranteed annual income argue that in a country with the collective wealth of the United States, access to such basic
necessities should be considered a natural right of all citizens. This may
sound like a pipe dream to us today, but it is something that has been
considered on a number of occasions here in the United States. In 1969,
for example, President Richard M. Nixon proposed a guaranteed annual
income in the form of his Family Assistance Plan, legislation that he continued to push for throughout his first term in office. This plan would have
replaced the various "welfare" programs with direct cash payments and
would have included the working poor. The amount of the guaranteed
annual income proposed by President Nixon, $1,600 a year for a family of
four, translates into 2013 dollars as between $9,800 and $24,500, depend-
ing on the method used.[58] While the Family Assistance Plan had a lot of
support from respected economists such as John Kenneth Galbraith, it
faced strong resistance from vested interests in the system (caseworkers
and administrators), organized labor (which saw it as a threat), and those
who were simply unwilling to entertain the idea of providing income to
someone who was not actually working.[59]

When the Family Assistance Plan was proposed in the 1960s, Galbraith
estimated that it would cost around $20 billion (or $132 billion in 2013 dollars) to institute a guaranteed minimum income for all Americans. Such
an amount, he noted, was in the neighborhood of what we were spending
each year "to rescue freedom and democracy and religious liberty"[60] in
Vietnam. In 2012, we were spending nearly $700 billion on defense, which
is, after taking out the effects of inflation, more than five times the amount
noted by Galbraith.

In advocating for a guaranteed minimum living income, Dr. King was
responding to the ineffectiveness of efforts to eliminate poverty by addressing the consequences of poverty rather than poverty itself. He criti-

cized programs designed to improve housing and education, and to end hunger and violence, as not getting at the source of the problem, which is simply that too many people do not earn enough money to make ends meet. "I am now convinced," wrote Dr. King, "that the simplest approach will prove to be the most effective—the solution to poverty is to abolish it directly by a now widely discussed measure: the guaranteed income."[61] He was convinced that "in a nation which has a gross national product of $750 billion a year [1968 figures], it is morally right to insist that every person have a decent house, an adequate education, and enough money to provide basic necessities for one's family."[62] "We are likely to find," he noted, "that the problems of housing and education, instead of preceding the elimination of poverty, will themselves be affected if poverty is first abolished."[63]

The piecemeal approach to eliminating poverty is not only ineffective, it puts an undue burden on the people living in poverty, who must navigate elaborate and often incomprehensible government systems to get housing, food, clothing, health care, education, and other basic necessities. At the same time, it treats people as incapable of directing their own lives and communities and, through controlling what resources flow into a community, actually creates the problems it purports to solve. In his book *Chain of Change,* community activist Mel King provides detailed descriptions of how this system has worked in Boston to impoverish and disempower communities of color.[64] Martin Luther King Jr. argued that once people had the means to make decisions about their own lives, many of the scourges of poverty would disappear as people invested in what they needed for their families to live healthy lives. It is an arrogant and patronizing system that presumes to know what people need better than they themselves do.

Dr. King was aware of the fact that substituting a guaranteed income for piecemeal approaches to eliminating poverty would require a major overhaul of our priorities and the way we view people living in poverty. More importantly, it would require a shift in values, as Dr. King put it, "from a thing-oriented society to a person-oriented society."[65] There is a prevailing fear that if people are provided with a base income, they may squander it. While surely some may do so, cash-transfer studies conducted in other countries have consistently shown that when those living in poverty are provided with cash resources, they invest them in improving the lives of their families.[66] There is no reason to expect that it would be different in the United States.

It is true, times have changed. The U.S. population has grown from roughly 200 million in 1968 to over 300 million in 2010. But so has the national wealth, recessions notwithstanding. In 1968, the per capita gross domestic product (GDP) in the United States was $18,028; in 2010 it had risen to $37,330.[67] The 2010 figure is more than double that for 1968. All of which is to say that Dr. King's proposal for a guaranteed minimum living wage is at least as feasible today as it was when he proposed it in 1968.

The political climate has, however, become far less conciliatory, if not outright hostile, toward those who find themselves in the grips of poverty. The idea that "there but for the grace of God go I" has been edged out by a widespread belief that people living in poverty are responsible for their own plight and therefore have no claim on collective resources. This is a convenient belief for those who do not wish to share the national wealth.

While the guaranteed minimum income never made it off the ground, the earned income tax credit (EITC), established in 1975, is an attempt to address some of the same issues. It does this by reducing the tax burden on lower-income working families. Based on how many children are in the household and on total household income, the IRS sets an earned income tax credit that is applied to the tax due; in cases where the credit is more than the tax owed, the balance is refunded to the household. This program has kept millions of families afloat. In 2011, the IRS estimated that more than 26 million citizens benefited from the EITC. However, the EITC, unlike an across-the-board guaranteed income, requires that people file taxes, something that many low-income people don't do because they don't meet the income requirements for filing or because they are not aware of the program. The IRS estimates that in 2011, 20 percent of those who qualified for the EITC did not claim the credit.[68]

In addition to the idea of a guaranteed minimum living income, Dr. King urged that the minimum wage be a living wage. "There is nothing," Dr. King wrote, "but a lack of social vision to prevent us from paying an adequate wage to every American citizen, whether he be a hospital worker, laundry worker, maid or day laborer."[69] There is nothing wrong with requiring employers to pay their workers a decent wage on which they can live. Yet many of the salaried jobs lost during recent recessions have been replaced largely by service sector jobs, many of which pay at or near the minimum wage. According to the Bureau of Labor Statistics, in 2011 1.7 million American workers age sixteen and older were paid at exactly the federal minimum wage of $7.25/hour; 2.2 million were paid at hourly wages *below* the federal minimum wage.[70] Many of the available jobs, although they pay the mandated minimum wage, do not pay enough to cover food, shelter, health care, and clothing.[71] The result: the spectacle of so many people working two and three jobs and still not being able to make ends meet, not to mention the legions who have no work at all. It doesn't have to be this way.

The federal minimum wage was established in 1938. The relationship of minimum-wage income to poverty level has been steadily declining over the past several decades. The minimum wage has not kept pace with the growth of the economy or inflation. The 2009 mandated federal minimum wage of $7.25/hour provides an income of $1,256 a month or $15,080 a year for full-time work. This is 35 percent below the 2012 federal poverty line for a family of four, which is set at $23,050 per year. A full-time worker would have to earn $11.06/hour to rise above the poverty line. The poverty line is considered to be the rock bottom threshold below which families are lacking the resources to meet the basic needs for healthy living such as food, shelter, and clothing. The poverty line itself has been called into question as being based on outdated criteria that do not adequately reflect the real costs of living. For example, communications—telephones and computers—the costs of which were not relevant when the line was established more than half a century ago, are now considered essential expenses. And in many parts of the country—especially our cities—where the cost of living is particularly high, living at the poverty level would preclude the basic necessities of food and shelter, plus such basic things as heat and hot water, electricity, health care, transportation, laundry, and so on. Even in less expensive cities and rural areas, the cost of living still surpasses what one can earn at minimum wage. According to the National Low Income Housing Coalition,[72] there is no state in the nation where a minimum-wage worker can afford a two-bedroom unit at fair market rent, working a standard forty-hour work week. This means that a single parent working a minimum-wage job does not earn enough to pay for suitable housing for

his or her family. Nor will he or she have anything left for such basic necessities as food, health care, transportation, utilities, laundry—never mind
child care. A minimum-wage job simply does not bring in enough income
to live on. An inadequate minimum wage is in fact part of the "edifice that
produces beggars" that Dr. King urged us to restructure.

Barbara Ehrenreich's 2001 book, *Nickel and Dimed: On (Not) Getting
By in America,* bears witness to the challenges of making it on low-wage
jobs. From 1998 to 2000, Ehrenreich worked a series of low-wage jobs, setting herself the task of "getting by" on what she earned. In the book, she
shares her experiences and provides an inside view of life on the edge, the
extra costs of being poor, and the impossibility of getting by on minimum
wages. She concludes that the poor, rather than being supported by the
largesse of the rich as is so often claimed, are actually supporting the rich
by doing their housekeeping, cooking, and child care for wages so low as
to preclude getting by in any reasonable sense of the term. In 2012, the
Economic Policy Institute estimated that one-quarter of all workers in
the United States held low-wage jobs (clerks, housekeepers, wait staff)
like those Ehrenreich worked.[73]

Many in the middle class are not aware of what Ehrenreich quickly realized: it is expensive to be poor. It's not just that people living in poverty
have less money to pay for basic necessities; basic necessities for the poor
actually cost more. Renters do not benefit from the mortgage interest de-
duction, nor do their monthly payments of rent count toward ownership
of land or housing that they can draw on in times of need. Even becoming
a renter is problematic on minimum wage; there are security deposits and
often first and/or last month's rent to put up before one can even think
of renting an apartment or house. Food is more expensive, as well. Poor
neighborhoods typically have few if any full-service grocery stores, and
the convenience stores that are present are notorious for their high prices
and their limited offerings of fresh produce and healthy foods. To benefit
from the lower costs and higher quality offered by large supermarkets
requires traveling distances that entail extra cost in time and transportation. People working minimum-wage jobs (or two or three) don't have
the time or money to do this. Laundry presents similar financial and time
constraints since many people who rent do not have access to their own
washer and dryer and must go to a commercial self-serve laundry. For a

family of four this is expensive in money as well as time. Finally, there's the burden of consumer debt. Low- and middle-income earners are making up, when they can, for falling incomes by using credit, thereby becoming what Kevin Phillips, in his book *American Theocracy*, termed "modern day indentured servants."[74] All of this is particularly true for African Americans and other racially/culturally marginalized groups.

A major issue for those trapped in the kinds of low-wage service jobs Ehrenreich describes is that they have little or no collective bargaining power, unionization in this sector being extremely low. Strong labor unions, for which Dr. King strongly advocated, provide a way for workers to have a say in setting the terms of their work—pay, hours, safety, benefits—through collective bargaining. Yet, the systematic evisceration of labor unions that has taken place in the United States since the 1980s is a major contributing factor to the shrinking number of living-wage jobs and increasing income and wealth inequality.

Dr. King was a staunch advocate of workers' rights, and in particular the right of workers to band together to make certain demands of their employers and to use the power of the strike, or work stoppage, to back up their demands. As such, he was concerned with building the union movement and the power of employees to have a say in the workplace. He also worked closely with unions on larger political issues that affected workers' lives; labor unions were active in both the civil rights movement and the antiwar movements of the 1960s and 1970s. It is telling that Dr. King spent his last few days on earth standing in solidarity with striking sanitation workers in Memphis, Tennessee, and that it was in the course of this support for labor that he was assassinated.

Over the course of the last quarter of the twentieth century, labor unions lost the clout they once had, leaving large parts of the labor force at the mercy of employers for whom worker safety and well-being often take a back seat to profit. This downward spiral in the power of labor is often traced to the dramatic 1981 destruction of the air traffic controllers' union, PATCO (Professional Air Traffic Controllers Organization). In the years leading up to the strike, as air travel had become more popular, the job of the air traffic controller had become a notoriously stressful one. Yet PATCO had been a strong union that had, through negotiation and strike actions, managed to enforce certain safety standards and secure decent working conditions and wages for its workers. In August 1981, faced with escalating volume in their workload, air traffic controllers went out on strike to demand a shorter work week, pay increases, and earlier retirement. The strike, which had an immediate effect on airlines' bottom lines, was declared illegal by President Ronald Reagan, who ordered the nearly 13,000 striking PATCO workers back to work on pain of losing their jobs. Most held out, and, indeed, just two days into the strike, the 11,345 strikers who refused to return to work were summarily fired—and banned forever from federal employment. This had, and has continued to have, a chilling effect on labor. Fewer people are willing to strike for decent wages and working conditions when the result may well be no job at all.

In recent standoffs with labor, it has been the government at both federal and state levels that has led the attack. We have seen the enactment of "right to work" laws in a number of states, often at the behest of governors. These laws, by outlawing obligatory union dues, are putting an end to the "union shop," which derived much of its bargaining strength from the fact that all workers in a shop were part of the union. There are now twenty-four states with right to work laws. In highly contentious cases in Wisconsin, Ohio, Michigan, and Indiana, public workers such as teachers were stripped of their rights to organize. In Ohio, voters fought back, repealing the governor's law banning strikes; in Wisconsin, after massive demonstrations, Governor Scott Walker's legislation curtailing worker's rights was struck down by the courts as violating the state constitution.

The result of this systematic destruction of unions is that workers have less and less say in the conditions under which they work. Dr. King was convinced that the right to organize and to collectively bargain for decent working conditions and living wages was key to ensuring that workers would not be exploited by profit-hungry employers. Over the course of his public life, Dr. King delivered an impressive number of speeches to union groups.[75] In April 1968, in Memphis, where he had gone to support striking sanitation workers, Dr. King delivered his last public speech. In it, he urged striking workers to insist not only on decent wages and working conditions, but on the right to organize. "We can get more together," he said, "than we can apart."[76]

The power of organized labor has steadily declined since its high point in the 1950s, when some 40 percent of workers were covered by union contracts; by 2012 just over 11 percent of the labor force was unionized. According to figures released in early 2013 by the Bureau of Labor Statistics, over the past thirty years, union membership has dropped from over 20 percent to 11.3 percent, the lowest level in almost a century. Union membership figures for all occupations declined from 2011 to 2012. Those in sales and "related occupations" had the lowest level of unionization, at 3.5 percent. Teachers, police and fire, allied health care workers, and those in the public sector tend to have the strongest unions, but even these hover below 40 percent membership, all down from 2011 levels. In 2011 and 2012, collective bargaining came under attack in a number of high-profile cases aimed at further curtailing the power of unions to represent public sector workers. The long-term effect has been a precipitous decline in workers' rights to collective bargaining and a shrinking number of jobs that pay a living wage. This same report notes that in 2012 the median weekly income for full-time union workers was $945; for nonunion workers it was $742; that's a difference of nearly $10,000 a year.[77]

This decline in the power of collective bargaining can be traced to loss of jobs in the manufacturing sector, which was once the stronghold of organized labor, and to increased government regulation of the workplace. The weakening of the manufacturing sector is at least partly the result of the jobs having gone elsewhere, as countless companies packed up and moved their operations to "right-to-work" states that are hostile to unions and their demands for living wages, or out of the country entirely—where there may be few or no regulations on employers.

A second factor is that the role of unions in regulating the workplace has been at least partially taken over by government through the Occupational Safety and Health Administration (OSHA), and through laws prohibiting discrimination and governing such things as safety, hours worked, overtime, and health coverage. Whether government oversight of health and safety is as effective as worker oversight was certainly called into question by the 2013 explosions at the fertilizer plant in West, Texas, where 15 people were killed and more than 160 injured, not to mention the dozens of homes, businesses, and public buildings that were destroyed. The plant had been last inspected by OSHA in 1985—nearly thirty years prior—and at the time had been cited for safety violations. Government regulation of the workplace is clearly not a replacement for employee oversight through unions. After all, who, if not workers, have the biggest stake in making sure their workplaces are safe?

Dr. King supported labor unions because they assure that there is a degree of democratic participation in the workplace and that workers have a voice—in how they are paid, in the conditions under which they work, and more generally, on larger political issues affecting their lives.

Another major concern of Dr. King was the societal distribution of resources. During his lifetime, concentration of national wealth at the top had not reached the extremes we are witnessing today. In the 1960s and 1970s, the share of national income going to the top 1 percent of the population was around 9 percent; in 2007 it was over 23 percent, and while it dipped during the 2007–2009 recession, it was back up and nudging 25 percent by 2011.[78] Yet, even in his time, Dr. King saw the skewed distribution of wealth as an indicator of the materialism that kept so many Americans in poverty. In a prescient 1957 address at the Highlander School, he warned about an "economic system which takes necessities from the masses to give luxuries to the [upper] classes."[79] The decline in the power of organized labor has certainly been a factor in the increasing concentration of wealth at the top.

As noted above, the per capita GDP of the United States has risen from $18,028 in 1968 to $37,330 in 2010, more than doubling in around forty years. So where is all this wealth and why are there still so many Americans living in poverty? The Occupy movements that cropped up around the world in 2011 were on target when they talked about the 99 percent versus the 1 percent. The math is simple: if nearly one-fifth of the national income goes to just 1 percent of the population, this means that there's not much pie to go around for the remaining 99 percent—and perilously little for the more than 46 million people at the bottom who live at or below the official poverty line, often in spite of working one or more full-time jobs.

This trend toward greater and greater concentration of national wealth at the very top is having serious consequences for those at the bottom. From 2000 to 2011, at the same time that the American economy grew by more than 18 percent,[80] median income for working-age households actually *dropped* by 12.4 percent.[81] By 2010, more than 15 percent of the U.S. population—nearly one in six people—was living at or below the official poverty line, and long-term unemployment had reached the highest levels since records were first kept in 1948. Between 2006 (the year before the onset of the so-called Great Recession) and 2010, the proportion of people living in poverty increased by 27 percent. We hear a lot about the economic recovery, but what we don't hear is that only the rich are recovering. The fact is that the lion's share of the gains of the recovery have been going to the top 1 percent of the population: in 2010 the incomes of the top 1 percent grew by 11.6 percent while those for the bottom 99 percent grew by only 0.2 percent.[82] This would be of great concern to Dr. King.

So far, we've been looking at income, that is, what one earns from working, interest, dividends, rents, and royalties. Wealth is another matter; it refers to everything one owns—such as land, homes, stocks, boats, and other property—minus one's debts. As noted earlier, wealth and income are not synonymous. Inheritance, or what parents are able to leave to their children—often as a result of what their parents and parents before theirs were able to leave—is a significant consideration here. When we look at wealth distribution—as opposed to income distribution—the picture is even more extreme: the top 10 percent of the U.S. population now controls nearly 75 percent of national wealth, while the 50 percent at the bottom together control just over 1 percent.[83]

If we look into wealth distribution by race, the conclusion that racial inequality is alive and well is unavoidable. A 2013 study by the Brandeis University Institute on Assets and Social Policy found that from 1984 to 2009, even though black college graduation rates tripled and more black Americans were elected to public office at all levels, the wealth gap between whites and blacks nearly tripled.[84] The study attributed this to a range of things, the most important being the legacy of housing discrimination through restrictive covenants, redlining (demarcating certain neighborhoods as poor mortgage risks), and the subprime lending scandals that cost many African Americans their homes. As homeownership is one of the main ways that people in the United States have built wealth, the historic exclusion of African Americans from the housing market has been a major factor in the racial wealth gap.

Tax policies have an important function in terms of redistributing resources more equitably than the market is able to do and assuring the collection of funds for public works, defense, and social programs. Over the years, tax policies have shifted the burden of public financing from those with the most resources to those with the least. This practice, coupled with a prevailing ethos that extols profit and considers those who get left by the wayside as collateral damage, has seriously compounded the problem of resource distribution. These are major changes that have taken place since Dr. King's time.

While there have been promising signs in terms of tax code revisions, the federal tax system still overwhelmingly favors the wealthy and corporations. Corporate income tax, capital gains tax rates, and marginal tax rates have followed a downward trend over the past several decades. Corporate income tax as a share of GDP has fallen from 6 percent in the 1950s, to 4 percent in 1968, to a low of 1 percent in 2009.[85] The tax on capital gains (on profits from the sale of property or other investments), which hovered around 40 percent in the late 1970s, had dropped to 15 percent in 2003, where it stayed through 2009.

Federal income taxes increase progressively as income increases. There are currently six tax brackets, and income in each bracket is taxed at a different rate. In 2012, tax rates for a person filing as head of household were set at 10 percent for the lowest bracket of income (up to $12,400), to 35 percent for the sixth, or highest, bracket (over $388,350). Marginal income tax rates (that is the rate assessed on the top brackets of income) have dropped from around 70 percent in the 1960s and 1970s to a low of 35 percent in 2012. The effect of these changes is that higher-income earners are paying far less than they were fifty years ago. Again, there are promising signs that this may be changing; as of 2013, the rate on the top chunk of income was reset to 39.6 percent. But this is still a long, long way from where we were in the 1970s.

Payroll taxes, on the other hand, have risen. Payroll taxes are assessed on earned income (wages, salary, business earnings); they are not assessed on unearned income such as investments, rental income, and inheritances. Of critical importance in understanding the unequal impact of payroll taxes is the fact that the highest-earning segment of the population earns less of its income from payroll taxable work than others do (they are more likely to have investment income, rental income, and so on). This means that lower-income workers are paying a larger chunk of their income to the collective pot than are the high rollers. Payroll taxes are assessed as a percentage of earnings, and include the Social Security tax and the Medicare tax, along with various other state-mandated payroll taxes. As of 2013, the employee share of federal payroll taxes—taxes that fund Social Security and Medicare—was 7.65 percent of gross income. Payroll taxes are not only a high percentage of low-wage workers' incomes, but they are unequally leveled on rich and poor. If a person earns over \$113,708, he or she pays no Social Security taxes on anything above this amount.

Over the last several decades, there has been a growing acceptance of vast inequities in income. Whereas in Dr. King's day, it was virtually unheard of for a CEO to earn more than twenty-five times more than his or her workers, as we move into the second decade of the twenty-first century, CEOs frequently earn some two hundred times more than their workers. This kind of income inequality—fueled by shrinking wages, growing unemployment, and tax policies that favor the rich—has meant that the growth of our economy has not had much benefit for the vast majority of Americans.

There seems to be a general feeling that issues of distribution are best left to the "market," which we have been led to believe will, over time, equalize things. But as Massachusetts Institute of Technology economist Erik Brynjolfsson noted, "there is no economic law that says technological progress has to benefit everybody or even most people. It's possible that productivity can go up and the economic pie gets bigger, but the majority of people don't share it."[86] This is precisely what has been happening over the last several decades: the pie has grown, but the benefits of this growth have gone to those at the very top. In fact, the share of the pie for the bottom half of the population has shrunk.

As a nation, we do have the resources to take seriously the well-being of all of our people, but the question is whether we have any interest in doing so. It's up to those of us who care about fairness to advocate for government policies that ensure that the nation's resources are more equitably distributed. We need to understand that, contrary to popular theories, this is not something the "market" is equipped to do.

In terms of economic justice, Dr. King also advised us to rethink the level of our investments in the military. He argued that a secure society is one that makes it a priority to assure that collective wealth is distributed so that everyone can be assured of the basics and no one need live in abject poverty. In a speech to labor delivered in March 1968, when the

United States was heavily involved in Vietnam, he said, "I'm afraid that our government is more concerned about winning an unjust war in Vietnam than about winning the war against poverty right here at home."[87] If, as suggested earlier, we replace the war in Vietnam with the War on Terror, we see that in terms of national priorities, we are in a similar place. As a nation, we have chosen to allocate the bulk of our national resources to defending our country from foreign enemies, increasingly at the expense both of alleviating poverty and investing in infrastructure like transportation and education systems. The 2012 defense budget was nearly $700 billion, by far the largest single piece of the U.S. budget pie. It is time to rethink the meaning of national security: Is a country really secure when more than 15 percent of the population live in poverty and one in four children goes to bed hungry? Is not widespread poverty as much an enemy to our democracy as the external threats we spend so much money addressing?

Finally, Dr. King was an advocate of job creation as a way of assuring living wages to a wider segment of the population. It would certainly be in our national interest to create jobs—we have a lot of unemployed people looking for work, and at the same time an enormous amount of work that needs to be done to repair our crumbling infrastructure. In contrast to Dr. King's era, we are now facing a situation where critical infrastructure such as roads, bridges, the electrical grid, communications networks, and water supply systems are in dangerous disrepair. A 2013 article in the *New Yorker*[88] on the destruction caused by Hurricane Sandy in the Rockaways points to the fragile condition of much of our infrastructure for electricity and communications.

We might do well to look back at the Works Progress Administration (WPA) of the 1930s. The WPA was a massive public works project created in April 1935 by executive order of President Franklin D. Roosevelt in the wake of the Great Depression, when unemployment had reached 25 percent. It was aimed at putting Americans back to work, and in its eight years of operation, it created some eight million jobs building airports, hospitals, courthouses, libraries, schools, post offices, bridges, roads, parks, and dams; documenting American life; and creating public art. An important aspect of the WPA was its inclusion of creative workers; the Federal Writers Project was responsible for recording first-person narratives of men and women coping with the Depression, customs of various ethnic groups, and some 2,300 oral histories of former slaves. These narratives serve as a corrective to our societal denial of the terrible and continuing impact of slavery and would surely have been lost forever had it not been for the Federal Writers Project. Another arm of the WPA was the Federal Art Project, which employed some 6,600 artists—musicians, actors, and visual artists—who made more than 200,000 pieces of public art in the form of posters, paintings, and murals—many of which can be seen in post offices and courthouses across the country. The Federal Art Project's *Index of American Design* was a massive project documenting the practical and fine arts of all regions of the country. Today, the legacy of the WPA is everywhere; it would be hard to put a value on its enormous contributions to the material and cultural life of the United States.

The initial budget for the Works Progress Administration was $35 million (roughly $586 million in 2013 dollars). Over its eight years of operation, during which it employed more than eight million people, the WPA cost the US government about $27.5 billion per year in 2013 dollars. Recall that the 2012 budget for defense was around $700 billion. All of which is to say that a massive public works program along the lines of the WPA could easily be financed through redirection of a portion of our military spending and reform of the tax system.

As we will see in the next chapter, if things are looking rough for Americans as a whole, the aggregate data hide the fact that things are significantly worse for African Americans and other racially and culturally marginalized groups. The overall poverty rate may be 15 percent, but for African Americans it is 25 percent, or one in four people. While economic injustice is just one of the ways racism operates, Dr. King was convinced that racism is a problem that "cannot be solved unless the whole of American society takes a turn toward greater economic justice."[89]

In this time of concentration of wealth and income at the top, stagnating wages, outsourcing of jobs, automation, the decline of company-provided health and retirement benefits, and the decreasing leverage of workers to demand living wages due to the systematic dismantling of unions, Dr. King's warnings about rampant materialism are more pertinent than ever before. Gains occasioned by programs introduced during the 1960s' War on Poverty are quickly being eroded. As our focus has been directed away from those living in poverty and toward the illusory "middle class," the programs that have provided a degree of protection for the most vulnerable are now under attack. We owe it to ourselves and to the memory of Dr. King to protect whatever gains have been made, reverse spiraling inequality, and work toward a society that honors everyone—both here at home and in the global community.

RACISM

There must be a recognition on the part of everybody in this nation that America is still a racist country. Now however unpleasant that sounds, it is the truth. And we will never solve the problem of racism until there is a recognition of the fact that racism still stands at the center of so much of our nation and we must see racism for what it is.

Martin Luther King Jr., from "The Other America,"
address delivered at Grosse Pointe, Michigan, March 1968

The first step toward eliminating racism is to acknowledge its existence, something this country has yet to do in any serious way. There is an astounding level of denial about racism and the central role it plays in all of our institutions. Given how obvious the effects of racism are, the continuing denial suggests a societal delusion of great proportions. We would like to have racial justice and be done with a damning past, but we don't want to do any of the things that would move us in this direction. We persist in coming up with other explanations, some more outlandish than others, to explain the huge racial inequities that run throughout all levels of our society. Until we get past this denial and face the facts, we can't expect to make any progress. We are not going to eliminate racism by pretending it doesn't exist. A "colorblind" society is not necessarily a racially just one.

It is important to realize that racism is deeply implicated in the scourges of militarism and materialism. It undergirds the belief that some are more deserving than others, that it is okay to visit violence on certain "others," be that the violence of drone attacks or the withholding of a fair share of the earth's resources. While Dr. King focused much of his attention on the United States, he was well aware that racism was a global problem. "Racism," he said, "is no mere American phenomenon. Its vicious grasp knows no geographical boundaries. In fact, racism and its perennial ally—economic exploitation—provide the key to understanding most of the international complications of this generation."[90]

I am defining racism as a social system in which "race" is a major organizing principle. (The fact that the notion of "race" has no biological basis does not prevent it from having enormous sociological and political significance.) A racist society is one in which social goods are systematically distributed along racial lines. Another and perhaps more accurate term is "white supremacy," since it is white people as a group who have the corner on society's resources. We have a distributional system based on a hierarchy determined by one's "race." A look at statistics for any number of social goods (education, employment, health, wealth, housing, among other things) clearly reveals the hierarchy, with white people as a group doing the best and black people (and certainly American Indians) doing the worst, with various other groups in between. This is not to ignore the fact that there are a lot of white people who are doing poorly or that there are some black people who are doing well. But when we look at the big picture, clear patterns emerge that are hard to explain away (although many persist in trying).

As Dr. King so clearly put it, "A society that has done something special *against* the Negro for hundreds of years must now do something special *for* him in order to equip him to compete on a just and equal basis."[91] Dr. King's proposals were aimed at finding ways to repair the damage wrought by centuries of "special treatment" of African Americans. We are accustomed to thinking of special treatment as positive, but this is not what Dr. King had in mind. This "special treatment" began when Africans were first brought to this country in chains and has continued in various forms up into the present. This has entailed receiving second-class education; being excluded from voting and civic participation and from large sectors of the job market; having limited access to public facilities such as hospitals, transportation, and recreational facilities; being banned from white neighborhoods and entire towns; being refused FHA loans, the benefits of the GI Bill, farm loans, and extension services; being subject to unethical scientific experimentation such as the infamous Tuskegee syphilis study; being excluded from hotels, restaurants, and other commercial spaces; being incarcerated at much higher rates than whites; and

being subject to white terrorism and murdered with impunity—individu-
ally in the case of lynching, or as whole communities as in the case of 1921
Greenwood massacre in Tulsa, Oklahoma. Or more recently in Philadel-
phia, when in 1985, in an effort to "rein in" what it saw as a disruptive group,
the city dropped a bomb on a house in an African American neighborhood
and then intentionally let the whole neighborhood go up in flames. The
damage has been cumulative; each generation inheriting the injuries and
setbacks of the one that went before.

Dr. King was talking about reparations. He was not talking about cash
payments to individuals, but about putting government resources into
building communities that have been neglected by centuries of marginalization and exclusion. We do associate Dr. King with the fight to end
racism. But our recollections focus almost entirely on his role in ending
legal segregation. The civil rights movement was successful in changing
laws (although Dr. King was well aware of the gulf between legislation
and its implementation), but this was only the tip of the iceberg. "The real
cost lies ahead. . . . The discount education given Negroes will in the future
have to be purchased at full price if quality education is to be realized.
Jobs are harder and costlier to create than voting rolls. The eradication of
slums housing millions is complex far beyond integrating buses and lunch
counters."[92] Dr. King was clear that it would take a massive infusion of
resources, human and material, into African American communities to
reverse the drain of resources that has been ongoing since the arrival of the
first Africans on our shores. This drain has effectively kept the American
dream out of reach for most African Americans. As long as economic inequality prevents people from taking advantage of the gains made by the
civil rights movement, he noted, these gains are meaningless.

It is a sign of our selective memory that this call for reparations does
not figure in our recollections of Dr. King. Nevertheless, it is clear that
reparations are what he was talking about. Dr. King called on us to repair hundreds of years of special treatment against African Americans,
to redress, in his words, "the economic depression caused by centuries of
deprivation."[93] He knew that this would require not only billions of dollars but a complete transformation of the way we think and the way we
do business. And he was well aware that this would be a hard pill to swal-
low for white people, even for those who were his supporters. He urged

white Americans—individuals, groups, and agencies—"to rise above the hypocrisies of the past and begin to take an immediate and determined part in changing the face of their nation."[94]

Racism—or white supremacy, the beliefs and systems designed to benefit whites and keep them in an advantaged position—is deeply embedded in our country's history. Dr. King reminded us of our national beginnings in a "form of racism that was relentlessly pursued on American shores: the physical extermination of the American Indian."[95] The systematic destruction of a whole people on whose land the United States was built, its cultivation by the forced labor of enslaved Africans, the railroads built by Chinese laborers to move the goods produced, and the continuing exploitation of immigrant labor reveal a pattern of using racialized "others" to build our national wealth. While Dr. King was talking primarily about African Americans, he was mindful of the many other groups that have been marginalized and excluded—including poor whites—whose labor, skills, and resources have been exploited to build an economy that continues to confer its benefits on very limited groups of white people.

In that sense, "white supremacy" is a useful term, as it puts the spotlight on the cause of the problem rather than on its consequences. The white-dominated academic and public policy communities have spent an inordinate amount of energy and expense searching for the roots of the problems that plague African American communities—everywhere except in the most obvious places. Researchers and scholars (most of them white) have proposed explanations such as the "failure of the black family," innate intelligence deficits, criminal culture, and the culture of poverty. Few have bothered to look at institutionally backed white culture and the role it has played in creating and fueling problems in the African American community.

A notable exception was the report of the President's National Advisory Commission on Civil Disorders, more commonly known as the Kerner Commission Report, issued in February 1968.[96] The Kerner Commission was established by President Lyndon B. Johnson to investigate the causes of the uprisings that took place in cities across the country in the mid-1960s and to make recommendations for addressing the causes. The authors essentially concurred with Dr. King's observation that in order to find the origins of the "Negro problem," it is necessary to look at the white man's problem. The commission pointed to white racism and persistent racial inequality as causes of the urban rebellions that had rocked major cities throughout the nation. Like Dr. King, the report's authors maintained that white America bore much of the responsibility. In their words, "What white Americans have never fully understood but what the Negro can never forget—is that white society is deeply implicated in the ghetto. White institutions created it, white institutions maintain it, and white society condones it."[97] The report decried the neglect and isolation of African Americans in run-down, economically abandoned inner cities and recommended job creation, increased social services, diverse and better-trained police forces, and massive investments in decent housing. Just over a month after the report was issued, Dr. King was assassinated and more than one hundred cities erupted in violence. The report was never acted upon.

During the 250-year period from the arrival of the first Africans in Jamestown in 1619 to the abolition of slavery in 1863 and beyond, Africans provided the labor on which the U.S. economy was built. One of the essential features of this was that those held in bondage were not paid. Moreover, their labor, their bodies, and their lives, down to the most intimate details, were controlled entirely by others. They brought not only labor; they provided expertise as well. English settlers, after all, were hardly experts in rice cultivation. It was Africans from the Senegambia and what is now Guinea Bissau and Sierra Leone who were the specialists in handbuilt irrigation canals and rain-fed upland rice production, engineering rice cultivation throughout the Carolinas and Georgia and amassing huge fortunes for plantation owners. Africans were also experts in indigo production, another major crop during the early period of slavery in the United States.

The industrial revolution with its mills humming away in river towns across New England would never have been possible without the cotton that was cultivated by enslaved Africans. The profits made from cotton and from the sugar plantations that fueled the Triangle Trade that enriched New England merchants, and from the skilled work of enslaved tradesmen—not to mention the enormous profits realized by insurance companies, banks, and other businesses that depended on the slave economy—provided the capital that permitted the nation to thrive economically. In this sense, we might think of reparations as a sort of back pay for centuries of unpaid labor and expertise. Moreover, in addition to labor and technical expertise, Africans brought many forms of music, healing arts, culinary traditions, languages, and customs—all of which have become proud parts of our collective culture.

Throughout the period of slavery, almost all Africans who were brought to the United States, their children, and their grandchildren (many fathered by white slave owners) were, by virtue of their African descent, deprived of all rights, including the rights to their own bodies.[98] This is something we need to face head-on. And we need to face the fact that the legacy of this history persists in the institutions of our nation today.

Too often in our self-flagellation over slavery we fail to make the connection between the suffering of generations of African-descended people and the enrichment of the nation's citizens who were, at the time, land-owning white men. Our focus on suffering Africans obscures the fact that slavery had a very clear purpose: it was designed to provide enormous benefits to the economy, an economy controlled by specific groups of white people. And while none of us here today were there at the time, we are all—recent immigrants included—the inheritors of this history. The benefits of this system have, over time, accrued in both institutional and personal terms, just as the disadvantage of being enslaved has been compounded in subsequent generations. It is disingenuous to pretend otherwise. If we are passively benefitting from racial injustice—past and present—and doing nothing to change the systems creating the problem, we are complicit with this history.

Moreover, we are incorrect to assume (or pretend) that the bad times for blacks ended at the close of the Civil War. Discrimination and violence against blacks continued to be the rule in the years that followed. The years from 1880 to 1918 saw an increase in attacks against rural blacks by white vigilantes; during that time, blacks were being lynched on an average of ten a week, including activity in northern as well as southern cities. To our national shame, of the nearly two hundred anti-lynching bills introduced in the U.S. Congress, the latest of these in 1952, not one was ever passed.

For the better part of the twentieth century, "Jim Crow" continued to constrain the lives of African-descended people in the United States through exclusionary laws and practices. In the 1950s, urban renewal facilitated the dismantling of hundreds of black neighborhoods throughout the country. The regular ridicule of black images in film, advertising, and elsewhere in the public sphere was commonplace. This included themes of blacks as lazy, as jungle savages, as sexually licentious, and as of lower intelligence. Nor are these things entirely in the realm of history.

Dr. King was clear that correcting this problem would require "extensive adjustments in the way of life of some of the white majority."[99] In short, there is a cost attached to achieving racial justice, and the cost is not inconsequential. He noted the ambivalence among the great majority of (white) Americans, whom he characterized as being suspended between two opposing attitudes: "They are uneasy with injustice but unwilling yet to pay a significant price to eradicate it."[100] If we are truly to make racial equality a priority, we have to be willing to put our money where our mouths are. We are not talking here about "handouts"; we are talking about what it will take to level the playing field, which is what racial justice is all about. Already in 1966, the assistant director of the Office of Economic Opportunity estimated the long-range cost of "repairs" as one trillion dollars. That was a huge amount at the time and an even more enormous amount now. Where would this kind of money come from? That is precisely the question we have to ask ourselves.

Where *would* it come from? How could we even begin to achieve racial equality without sacrificing our way of life? The answer, which lies in the question itself, may be unsettling and is perhaps a key to understanding why, as Dr. King put it, "[racial] equality is so assiduously avoided."[101] But unless we are willing to accept the fact that racial justice has a cost attached, our talk of racial justice in America is just that, talk. But, many would ask, are these costly efforts really necessary now? After all, times have changed: we have had a black president; numerous government offices are headed up by African Americans; Oprah Winfrey, one of the richest women in America and a cultural icon, is African American; African Americans are more present than ever in the arts; there are African American CEOs[102] and college presidents.[103] Clearly, we are making progress, aren't we?

Not much, as it turns out. These high-profile signs of progress at the top mask vast racial inequities running through all levels of our society. It is these inequities that must be addressed if racial justice is to be achieved. We must address our consistent reluctance to accept blacks and other non-whites as full-fledged American citizens, with attendant rights to move freely throughout the society. We do not see, yet, these as rights guaranteed under law as much as favors from the white majority population.

Today, there are two major interrelated ways in which racism operates to disenfranchise African Americans: in the disparate production of poverty among African Americans and the disparate production of African American prisoners. Neither is new; both have worked over time to prevent African Americans from accumulating wealth and power, and both have been operating to control African Americans since the abolition of slavery in 1863. But the mechanisms through which they work have morphed over time. Just as one mechanism is outlawed, another pops up to take its place.

The Production of Poverty

Poverty does not come out of nowhere; it is produced by policies and practices that deny people an education, deny them jobs, and deny them homes and access to other societal goods. Compared with the general population, African Americans as a group have significantly lower rates of educational attainment and employment. This is a result of systematic discrimination and is the cause of high rates of poverty and accompanying ill-health.

Racism, as manifested in the body, is nothing short of a public health disaster. A comparison of health indicators for African Americans and the general population reveals this in no uncertain terms. Infant mortality is higher among African Americans; chronic diseases like diabetes and heart disease are higher; rates of HIV/AIDS are higher; and life expectancy is lower.[104] While to some degree these disparities are consequences of the poverty that often accompanies racism, there is something else at work here that crosses social class. Researchers are increasingly pointing to the physiological effects on the body of the chronic stress that racism inflicts on its targets. Chronic stress creates changes in the hormonal system and wears down the body in ways that are complex and deadly.[105] Racism, in short, makes people sick. A racist society is unhealthy for whites as it is for blacks. Even if whites do not have to face it openly, nevertheless the violence and painful ambiguity of racism is internalized and perhaps surfaces in ways that we have yet to acknowledge, thus skewing our understanding of the wider costs of racism.

While poverty is rife in African American communities, it is true that over the past several decades there has been a growth in the black middle class. Those who made it that far were often the ones who were disproportionately targeted for subprime loans—something made possible by banking deregulation—and who have borne the brunt of the collapse of the housing bubble. Until relatively recently, African Americans were largely excluded from the housing market; banks wouldn't give them loans, and restrictive covenants meant that there were few places to buy. Then financing became easy and neighborhoods opened up, but foreclosures have meant that keeping those homes has been another matter altogether. Losing a home to foreclosure is more than losing the roof over one's head; it is losing one's credit rating, which in this day and age is a serious matter.

On all major measures of well-being, African Americans score significantly lower than the general population and much lower than whites. These statistics are an indictment of hundreds of years of racist policies and practices designed to keep the American dream out of the hands of African Americans.

According to Dr. King, a critical piece of dismantling racism will be a commitment to economic justice for everyone—not only African Americans, but everyone. "Dignity," Dr. King observed, "is corroded by poverty."[106] This is true for each of us, regardless of race, religion, national origin, age, sexual orientation, or ability. Until economic justice for everyone becomes a priority, efforts to "fix" the situation of African Americans will be doomed to failure. "In short," Dr. King wrote, "the Negroes' problem cannot be solved unless the whole of American society takes a turn toward greater economic justice."[107]

Disparate levels of poverty among African Americans make a mockery of claims that we are on a level playing field and have equal opportunities. Laws assuring civil rights, even if they were seriously implemented, do not correct the racial distribution of poverty. As President Obama, echoing Dr. King, said in a 2008 address to the NAACP, "it matters little if you have the right to sit at the front of the bus if you can't afford the bus fare; it matters little if you have the right to sit at the lunch counter if you can't afford the lunch."[108] In this sense, Dr. King was clear that solving the "race problem" would require not only reparations to parties injured by centuries of racial injustice, but an overall reorientation toward economic justice—the equitable distribution of society's goods. He was not suggesting that we ignore the gross poverty among whites and other groups, but that we reorient ourselves toward a system that honors all people by taking the steps to assure that *no one* is obliged to live the kind of impoverished life that so many Americans—black, white, and other—now live.

As we saw in the section on materialism, over 15 percent of Americans fell below the poverty line in 2010. This aggregate data hides the fact that African Americans, with a poverty rate greater than 25 percent, are among those suffering the most from poverty.[109] That is more than one in four people. The concentration of poverty among African Americans—the flip side of the concentration of wealth among whites—is not, as we are often led to believe, an act of God or evidence of moral inferiority, but a legacy of racism, a legacy that will not go away until we take direct measures to address it. Just as wealth begets wealth, poverty begets poverty. If you have the capital to invest in your and your children's lives, you'll have a brighter future than if you do not. In 2010, white Americans as a group had twenty-two times the wealth of black Americans.[110] But how did they get it? And why do black Americans have so little relative to whites in America?

The answer lies in a history about which many of us are ill-informed. Let's go back 150 years to 1863, the year of the Emancipation Proclamation, the executive order issued by President Abraham Lincoln on January 1 of that year. It declared free all those held in bondage in the ten states of the confederacy (about three million of the four million people enslaved in the United States at the time). It was only in December 1865, with the ratification of the Thirteenth Amendment to the constitution, that slavery was finally outlawed throughout the United States. By that time, four million African Americans, as they came to be known, had been released from slavery. We celebrate this as a great moment in freedom. But these newly liberated people were at an extreme disadvantage and not just because of racism: they had no resources—no food or shelter, no land, no money, often few skills, no education to speak of (it had been widely forbidden for slaves to learn to read and write), and they had few if any connections in the halls of power. The family, certainly one of the most important resources in any society, had been systematically broken up.

Among the conclusions of the final report of the American Freedmen's Inquiry Commission to the Secretary of War in May of 1864 was this: "The essential is that we secure to them the *means* [my emphasis] of making their own way; that we give them, to use the familiar phrase, a fair chance. If, like whites, they are to be self-supporting, then, like whites, they ought to have those rights, civil and political, without which they are but laboring as a man labors with hands bound."[111] The recommendations of this commission led to the establishment of the Bureau of Refugees, Freedmen and Abandoned Lands, established formally in 1865. It was disbanded just seven years later by Congress, leaving unrealized the goal of assuring this new population of citizens the resources and civil rights deemed necessary for them to be on equal footing with their white counterparts. The purpose of the Freedmen's Bureau was confounded by administrative infighting, underfunding, diverse political agendas in Washington, and the increasing disappointment and hostility of poor whites. Eventually, pressure from working-class and poor whites shifted the government's focus to concerns of the white population. The Freedmen's Bureau and other attempts to provide newly freed populations with the "means of making their own way" were thus short-lived. General Sherman's earlier promise of forty acres and a mule might have shown the way to a different and more egalitarian future, but the order was revoked by President Andrew Johnson shortly after he took office, and land that had been distributed to freedmen was returned to Southern planters. The period of Reconstruction held out the first of many opportunities the country has had to turn things around. Unfortunately, these opportunities, like subsequent ones, were opportunities not taken.

Reconstruction refers to the period from 1865 to roughly 1877, when there were active efforts to integrate the millions of newly liberated citizens into the economic and political life of the country. This was a period of great progress when thousands of freedmen were elected to local, state, and national office, and when voting rates among African Americans were very high. But these short-lived victories were soon overshadowed by the institution of Black Codes and what came to be known as Jim Crow laws, laws that excluded African Americans, on threat of violence, not only from elected office, but from gainful employment and from voting and civic life altogether. After Reconstruction came to an end, much of the land that had been redistributed to freedmen was confiscated and returned to white planters. At the same time, harsh local laws were instituted that required freedmen to return to former slave-master holdings to work there as sharecroppers, which many did well into the twentieth century, when there were massive migrations to urban areas in the North and West with the promise of jobs in thriving industrial centers. Yet, once the African Americans were there, restrictive covenants and other forms of housing discrimination assured that the bulk of these migrants and their children who came after them would be trapped in the decaying urban ghettos that Dr. King referred to in the 1960s as emotional pressure cookers.

But let's return to the years immediately following emancipation. At that time, there was an enormous demand for education among freedmen, who organized to establish and fund thousands of schools throughout the South, initially with help from the Freedmen's Bureau, and more meaningfully from certain religious associations, particularly branches of the Methodist and Baptist churches. However, white resistance to educating African Americans, manifested through violence directed at schools and teachers, halted the spectacular progress that was made in the few short years following emancipation. As resources were pulled out of these schools, separate systems were established by law for blacks and whites, with black schools receiving very little public support. Blacks, however, were equally taxed to support school systems. Newly freed populations did not have the resources to support universal education in their communities, nor were states or municipalities interested in doing so. In spite of the extraordinary work of African American communities and their many successes in setting up, funding, staffing, and running their own schools, the vast majority of African Americans continued to have far fewer educational opportunities than their white counterparts. Given that education is such a strong determinant of employment status, income, and resources, this failure to support education for African Americans, backed by racial violence, served as an effective way of maintaining white advantage in the job market. And it set the tone for the next one hundred years and beyond, continuing into the present century.

As with their initial push for quality schools in the years following emancipation, it was African Americans who were at the forefront of the school desegregation fight ninety years later. Having witnessed the disparate quality of white and black schools, the NAACP (the National Association for the Advancement of Colored People) had sponsored a number of cases involving school segregation. In 1954 these cases were brought together in the class action suit against the Topeka Board of Education known as *Brown v. Board of Education*. The actual *Brown* case combined five separate NAACP-sponsored cases from four states and the District of Columbia aimed at desegregating schools. The underlying belief was that if white and black children were in the same schools, they would receive comparable educations. The *Brown* ruling ordered the integration of schools and the dismantling of "separate but equal" systems of education. But, as Dr. King noted in regards to civil rights legislation, the passage of laws does not guarantee their implementation. The late legal scholar Derrick Bell put it most forcefully in his 2004 book *Silent Covenants,* when he said that the successful *Brown v. Board of Education* lawsuit did not eliminate racial segregation; it just made it illegal. Like programs that attack the symptoms of poverty rather than poverty itself, the *Brown* ruling addressed only the *symptoms* of the systemic underlying racism that pervades our society. Bell quotes Judge Robert Carter's 1968 reflections, looking back at *Brown v. Board of Education:* "Few in the country, black or white, understood in 1954 that racial segregation was merely a symptom, not the disease; that the real sickness is that our society in all of *its* manifestations is geared to the maintenance of white superiority."[112] Many have argued that, in fact, today we have a situation worse than before *Brown* in that the black education system, built up by African Americans in their own interests, was effectively dismantled after *Brown* by the firing of thousands of black teachers and the closing of schools that served African American communities. Black students were now at the mercy of predominately white-run school systems, where they remain today, often "tracked," overdisciplined, and otherwise excluded from the fruits of a good education. Another opportunity lost.

But even if African Americans had equal educational opportunities and were not prevented by threats of violence from taking advantage of them, the labor market was and continues to be stacked in favor of whites. Recent studies confirm that racial discrimination in hiring is widespread. A look at statistics on unemployment and wages among African Americans suggests that something is awry. Unemployment among African Americans rose from 13.2 percent in November 2012 to 14 percent in January 2013, more than double the rate for whites, which was 6.9 percent in December 2012.[113] These percentages do not take into consideration the million or so African Americans who are in prison. And for those who do have jobs, wage disparities continue to drive poverty in African American communities. A 2011 report by the U.S. Census Bureau reported that in 2010, median household income for black families was less than 60 percent of what it was for non-Hispanic white families.[114]

Predatory lending and the recent subprime mortgage scandals have had a severe economic impact on African Americans. Numerous studies have shown that a disproportionate share of subprime mortgage loans were made to black consumers. For many, this has meant loss of their homes; it has also destroyed credit ratings, something that will have long-term effects in terms of not only home ownership, but the ability to finance higher education for future generations. And so the vicious cycle continues.

A 2013 Brandeis University study found that in spite of apparent gains for African Americans, the wealth gap between whites and African Americans is growing. "Public policies play a major role in widening the already massive racial wealth gap and they must play a role in closing it," said Dr. Thomas Shapiro, director of the Brandeis Institute on Assets and Social Policy and a principal author of the report. "We should be investing in prosperity and equity, instead we are advancing toxic inequality. A U-turn is needed."[115]

There is no end to the examples that could be cited, as racism operates throughout our institutions and its effects are compounded from one generation to the next. Suffice it to say that the high rate of poverty among African Americans is the result of complex and intertwined factors stretching back in history. The same can be said for the significantly lower rates of poverty among white people.

The Production of Prisoners

The excessive imprisonment of African Americans, as Michelle Alexander reminded us in her 2010 book *The New Jim Crow: Mass Incarceration in the Age of Colorblindness*, has been a feature of U.S. society since right after the Civil War when it was common practice to arrest former slaves for minor infractions, charge them excessive fines, and then put them in prison until they could pay off their debt. Their economic situation being what it was, this effectively made them prisoners in perpetuity.[116] They were hired out to work on chain gangs, but since their debts grew faster than their wages, they found themselves once again, for all intents and purposes, enslaved. The pattern of jobless blacks being arrested on vagrancy charges and then hired out to businesses continued well into the twentieth century.

The situation in 2013 is not much different. We now have another system of re-enslavement that also involves the targeting of African Americans for arrest and detention. African Americans are being incarcerated in our jails and prisons at an unprecedented rate, one that far outweighs their relative numbers in the population. African Americans constitute 1 million of the 2.3 million people incarcerated in the United States. This is 43 percent, contrasting starkly with U.S. census figures, which indicate that African Americans comprise just 13.5 percent of the population. At the same time, the relaxation in laws governing convict labor has meant new levels of profit for businesses taking advantage of prison labor. And the private prison industry has become one of the fastest growing industries in the United States, with the number of private prisons in the United States increasing from five to one hundred in the course of the last ten years.[117]

Already the United States has the distinction of having the highest rate of incarceration in the industrialized world—even though violent crime rates have dropped significantly over the past two decades. The culprit is partially the War on Drugs, which has inordinately targeted African Americans, who are locked up at nearly six times the rate of whites. Disparate sentencing rules that mandated far more severe penalties for possession of drugs more prevalent in poor, black communities than for those commonly used by whites landed hundreds of thousands of African Americans in prison. Other forms of racism, including the often subconscious operation of stereotypes inherited from the histories discussed above, continue to ensure that blacks make up an inordinate proportion of the U.S. prison population. From 1988 to 1994, the number of young black prisoners aged eighteen to twenty-five increased 355 percent.[118] At the same time, the passage of state level "three strikes" laws and mandatory minimum sentencing laws in the 1990s translated into increasingly long sentences. According to Bureau of Justice Statistics, one in three black men can expect to spend time in prison during his lifetime. Nor is it just black men who are being caught up in the correctional system; one in one hundred black women are now in prison, as well. Latinos are rapidly closing the gap, with a preponderance of young adults and adolescents caught up in the system.

We know that prison involves isolation from the larger society; that is part of the deal. Violence and brutality should not be part of the deal. Yet once in prison, an inmate has a high probability of being exposed to violence—from other prisoners and from prison staff. The chances of being a victim of rape, gang violence, abuse by officers, and infectious disease are significantly higher in prison than on the "outside." Prisoners also face the mental health consequences of extended solitary confinement.

Over the past several decades, the notion of prison as rehabilitation has overwhelmingly been replaced by a highly punitive approach that has gone hand-in-hand with the massive expansion of the U.S. prison population. As opportunities for rehabilitation have dwindled, time inside rarely translates as time spent preparing for a productive life outside. About one-third of prisoners have not completed high school; being able to earn a GED while in prison significantly decreases recidivism rates and increases postrelease earning power, particularly for minority inmates. Yet only one-quarter of prisoners are enrolled in such programs.[119] The possibility of earning a college degree was another way that inmates could "turn their lives around." However, with the abolition of Pell Grants to state and federal prisoners in 1994, the number of colleges offering degree programs for prisoners fell from 350 prior to 1995 to a low of 12 in 2005.[120] (It is worth reminding ourselves that because inmates who earn college degrees are less likely to return to prison after release, it is actually cost-effective, given that it costs taxpayers as much as $60,000 a year to keep one person in prison.)[121] With the withdrawal of rehabilitative services, inmates who in the past could use their time in prison to gain useful skills and education are now likely to become part of a captive labor force for the many companies that contract with prisons. Furthermore, once they are released, former prisoners face policies that discourage education by rating employment above enrolling in school among criteria for ending probation.

Prisons and prison labor are a lucrative business. Prison populations are increasingly being tapped by private industry as a cheap and easy-to-control labor force. Private prisons are now among the highest-performing investments in the stock market. In the 1930s, the domestic commerce in prison-made goods was outlawed. However, in 1979, with the decline of labor unions, which had been a strong voice against competition from convict labor, the Prison Industries Enhancement Act, or PIE, made private use of convict labor permissible. Workers are to be paid the "prevailing wage," but this does not mean a good wage or a fair wage. Once room and board are deducted (as is the practice in some prisons), the hourly rate may come to zero. Private companies have been quick to take advantage of the convict workforce. Today, the names of the private corporations using convict labor read like a roll call of household names.[122] Prisoners work for computer companies, telephone companies, banks, and major retailers. They work in textile and apparel manufacturing, packaging, electronics, telemarketing, and numerous other fields. This increasingly includes backbreaking agricultural labor harvesting crops in extreme weather conditions.[123]

As well as the obvious negative effects of being imprisoned, there are side effects that fan out to affect families, friends, and entire communities. If being poor is expensive, it's even more expensive when you have a family member in prison. The legal costs, costs of communication (phone companies make a huge profit on calls to prisoners), travel costs, and the psychological costs of stigma, stress, worry, and powerlessness place a heavy burden on individuals, families, and the African American community as a whole. Ex-prisoners are required to pay monthly fees to probation offices around the country, and some prisons tabulate other costs to be charged to the prisoner, once released. These costs are borne disproportionately by African Americans across the social spectrum. In many neighborhoods, one is hard pressed to find an African American who does not have a relative in prison; one in fifteen black children has a parent who is incarcerated—in contrast to the figure of one in forty for the general population.[124]

The placement of prisons in poor, rural white communities is viewed as a way to provide jobs and public representatives for depressed communities. This makes the economic viability of these poor white communities dependent upon supporting a system that targets poor black communities. And locating prisons in these rural areas makes it easier for middle-class communities to ignore the problem of an out-of-control and racist prison system. This continues a long-standing pattern of pitting poor whites against blacks. In the 1970s busing crisis in Boston, for example, it was the impoverished and neglected neighborhood of South Boston that was put at the forefront of school desegregation, leaving those in wealthier white neighborhoods, which were not required to participate in busing, to decry the racism of Southie residents.

Mass incarceration is a major factor in the disenfranchisement of the African American community. The 1965 Voting Rights Act may have put an end to poll taxes and literacy tests, but they have been replaced by other equally effective mechanisms for keeping the ballot box out of the reach of African Americans; one of them is the production of felons. The War on Drugs launched in the 1980s has had an inordinate impact on African American communities; 56 percent of those in state prisons for drug offenses are African Americans.[125] Because drug offenses are considered felonies, in many states the ex-offender, having done his or her time, is barred from a wide range of jobs, social services, and voting—in some cases, forever. The Sentencing Project reports that 5.85 million voting-age Americans were barred from voting in 2010 due to criminal records—three-quarters of these had served their terms and were no longer imprisoned. In 2010, one of every thirteen African Americans of voting age had been stripped of the right to vote, a rate more than four times greater than for non–African Americans.[126]

When seeking to answer the question posed earlier about where money to fund reparations would come from, we might bear in mind the cost of our current corrections system, which comes in at more than $63 billion per year. This amount does not include the rest of the criminal justice system: courts, judges, attorneys and legal counsel, probation officers, clerks and administrative personnel. Surely, a good portion of the money it takes to run this broken system could be redirected to building up the communities it has had such a major role in destroying.

Racism, or white supremacy, is one of the corrosive forces that Dr. King urged us to confront. Racism is reactivated on a daily basis through an elaborate web of institutions—the education system, religious institutions, the justice system, the transportation system, housing, public safety, social services, to name a few—all of which work in their own ways to deny society's resources to those deemed outsiders. A system that concentrates societal goods among one group of people requires that these goods be actively denied to others—otherwise the system would not work.

This system has sufficiently developed over time to become a well-oiled machine that requires very little to keep it going—no more than the silence and complacency of the population. Its workings remain outside the field of vision for the vast majority of those who are not among its immediate casualties. This ignorance about the systems that create racial inequalities in our society facilitates the belief that ending racism is just a matter of "tolerance" and being nice to everyone. But being nice to everyone is not going to change the way our schools operate, the way our police forces and courts do business, or the way the job market operates. Dr. King was clear that eliminating racism is not a matter of being nice to everyone; it is a matter of changing the institutions that distribute society's resources.

Institutions have lives of their own and are resistant to change. If we are to transform them into institutions that serve everyone and not just the few, it will require major changes in our everyday behaviors and concerted efforts on the parts of each of us.

3

Why It Matters

Martin Luther King Jr. was truly a prophetic voice. He warned us about a number of forces that, if left unchecked, lead to an increasingly unjust and unstable world. We have chosen not to heed his messages and find ourselves in a state of growing crisis on a number of fronts, all of which have their origins in systems of injustice. History would suggest that, at some point, systems based on extreme injustice collapse. But whether the current system can survive is not really the question we should be asking ourselves. Rather, it is whether we want it to survive, if this is the kind of world we want to live in. If not, it is up to us to change it.

The election of Barack Obama as president of the United States was seen as the hallmark of a new era, evidence that we had made significant progress in realizing Dr. King's dream. Symbolically, this may have been true; however, our tendency to focus on the achievements of individuals obscures the workings of the larger system. We like to celebrate uplifting stories of people who have triumphed over difficult odds, reinforcing the idea that it is a question of individual effort. We tout multiculturalism and diversity, without asking why such approaches are necessary in the first place. We ignore the workings of the institutions that perpetuate a system that has the effect of marginalizing large portions of the population. Electing an African American president was certainly a milestone, but it has not significantly altered the institutions and values that characterize the United States.

Clearly, I believe that we should be paying attention to Dr. King's prescriptions. But who should be paying attention? The short answer is that all of us should—everyone. That said, I think there is a special and particularly urgent role for white people—particularly those of us who have most benefited from the system. The societal racism Dr. King fought against remains central to the crises our society is confronting in the early twenty-first century.

WHOSE PROBLEM? WHITE AMERICA'S
SPECIAL RESPONSIBILITY

A good many observers have remarked that if equality could come at once the Negro would not be ready for it. I submit that the White American is even more unprepared.

Martin Luther King Jr., *Where Do We Go from Here?*

The issues Dr. King talked about obviously concern all Americans. However, different people are concerned in different ways; a bank president (probably white) will be differently implicated than will a young man in jail on drug charges (probably black). A single mother trying to make ends meet working two jobs has a different relationship to Dr. King's message than a married woman with a professional degree. We all have our role to play in creating the kind of society Dr. King envisioned. When it comes to racism, however, white people have a special role to play. Dr. King's words about white people remain as relevant today as when he wrote them forty-five years ago.

Dr. King was clear that both the barriers to racial justice and the hope for overcoming them lie with white people of good faith. "[A] sound resolution of the race problem in America will rest with white men and women who consider themselves as generous and decent human beings."[1] He was deeply disappointed that so many of this group, which he referred to as "white liberals," had lost their energy when it became clear that continuing the struggle would entail disturbing their "tranquility" and sense of "order," and when it posed threats to their financial and cultural advantages. He noted the tendency to assume that racism and white supremacy exist only among the "unlettered, underprivileged and poorer class whites,"[2] when it was the acquiescence of the silent majority that allowed, and continues to allow, the existence and growth of blatant racial injustice.

This is not to discount the impressive work of many whites in the cause of racial justice. There are countless groups of white people around the country working together and with people of color to educate themselves and their peers and to challenge racist practices and policies. Still, their numbers pale as a proportion of the white population. It is still true that most of us are turning a blind eye to the racism that permeates our lives and all of our institutions. It is not, finally, the "rednecks" and "crackers" that are driving this; it is those of us who have been socialized not to notice and not to speak out, hoping that racism will go away if we are just "nice to everyone."

As Dr. King noted, "Even in areas where white liberals have great influence—labor unions, schools, churches, and politics—the situation of the Negro is not much better than in situations where they are not dominant."[3] The focus on the "aesthetics" of integration—in which people of color are scattered throughout overwhelmingly white institutions—is an aspect of what Dr. King saw as the tendency of whites to self-delusion. The claim that one has black friends, frequently offered as a credential of one's antiracist leanings, is meaningless if one is not fighting against the injustices that plague the communities of "one's friends." As Dr. King said, "Love that does not satisfy justice is no love at all."[4]

It's time we face the fact that "being nice" is not an adequate strategy for dismantling a system of injustice that has been growing and morphing in this country for hundreds of years. It's going to take more than that. We have to be willing to sit with feelings of discomfort and to dispassionately consider where we fit in. "It is time," Dr. King said, "for all of us to tell each other the truth about who and what have brought the Negro to the condition of deprivation against which he struggles today."[5] Who and what was he talking about? Are we as white Americans responsible? Dr. King's answer was a resounding yes: "To find the origins of the Negro problem, we must turn to the White man's problem."[6] This, according to Dr. King, is where the problem lies. Importantly, it is also where the hope for change lies.

Dr. King expressed dismay at white people's lack of effort *"to re-educate themselves out of their racial ignorance* [my emphasis]. It is an aspect of their sense of superiority that the white people of America believe they have so little to learn."[7] He talked about the need to pull back the curtain on white racism, to take it out of the closet and "strip it of its rationalizations."[8] This requires first being able to "see" it—which is the point of reeducating ourselves. African Americans and other people of color have been calling attention to racism for ages; it is time for the rest of us to step back, take a deep breath, open our eyes, and actually look around us. What we see may surprise us, disturb us, and frighten us. But we need to keep looking. And then we need to speak out about what we see. It is the silence of the majority of white people that keeps white supremacy in place; it is their voices that can demand the changes required to end it and to achieve racial equality.

Dr. King was aware of the fact that among white Americans there is enormous resistance to programs that promote racial equality. Many whites tend to see these programs as offering some kind of unfair advantage or handouts. Affirmative action policies, which were designed to level the playing field by providing access to those to whom it had been systematically denied, have been greeted with enormous resistance from whites. Such resistance ignores the fact that white Americans have long benefited from preferential access to housing, employment, education, and other social goods. At the same time that many whites denounced affirmative action, they continued to turn a blind eye to the "negative action" of systematic housing discrimination, discrimination in the criminal justice system, discrimination in the job market, and discrimination in the educational system. You don't hear whites bemoaning these disadvantages as unfair; it is only when it is a question of advantages that it suddenly becomes unfair. So it seems to be okay and somehow not unfair for African Americans and other racially marginalized communities to suffer severe economic disadvantage. What's unfair is when these groups are extended compensatory advantages.

This illogical reasoning, Dr. King suggested, is at least partly due to a collective "racial ignorance." Whites as a group are woefully ignorant of the history of racial oppression in this country and its current pervasiveness. James Baldwin's words, written back in 1963, remain poignantly applicable today: "[White people] are still trapped in a history which they do not understand; and until they understand it, they cannot be released from it."[9]

The current growth of interest in racism and "white studies" is a good sign, with its focus on the history of racial preference and racial oppression in the country. But we have only begun to scratch the surface of what will be necessary for white people to, as Dr. King put it, "re-educate themselves out of their racial ignorance." There is profound resistance to admitting our ignorance about racism. We are afraid to admit what we don't know and perhaps even more afraid of what we might find out if we looked. Most whites have been socialized to not talk about racism or learn about it—beyond saying that it is essentially a thing of the past. This ignorance of history—of how whites got to where they are today—their socialization as white people, and the segregated nature of their daily lives means that it is easy for them not to see racism. When you start to look into it, it can be an upsetting and destabilizing experience.

Having spent the last twelve years facilitating courses for white people on challenging racism, I have come to see this failure to learn, to face the facts, as rooted in a deep sense of insecurity and fear. These fears are fourfold: (1) the fear of facing ourselves and seeing who we really are; (2) the fear of losing advantages, especially in these precarious economic times; (3) fear of retaliation; and finally, (4) the fear that the problem is just too big.

Because whites are accustomed to seeing racism as disadvantage for others, they rarely look at how it operates as a system of advantage. When we look at things this way, many of what are considered to be "achievements" turn out to be the result of a long history of racial preference conferred through the legal system and enforced by local policies and practices. We need to rethink our belief in meritocracy: the belief that advantages and benefits are solely the result of hard work and aptitude, and that if other people would just work as hard as we do, they would surely reap the same benefits. When we start to examine the situation more closely, we are forced to consider that as smart, hard-working, and accomplished as some may be, there are other forces at work that have contributed to their good fortune. It is disturbing to have to consider that maybe a good part of one's accomplishments is due to "white advantage."

When we ask ourselves: Where did I grow up? Who were my friends/ my parents' friends? What schools did I attend? Did my family go on vacation and if so, where and who else was there? Did I go to college? Do I have a job; how did I get it? Where do I live? Do I own a home; if so, how was I able to buy it? Am I healthy? We find that our answers to these questions are highly influenced by race. The answers to each question would likely be quite different for white and black Americans. Yet, there is great resistance among whites to seeing their lives through the lens of race—partly, I believe, because what is revealed goes counter to the American myth of meritocracy and calls an individual's achievements into question. It also belies the notion of whiteness as "an absence of race," as the American "default" ethnic category.

The fact that many whites live very "white" lives is not an accident; it is the result of laws, policies, and private agreements that have been designed to keep it that way. But most whites are ignorant of the effects of the GI Bill, the Federal Housing Administration, the Federal Farm Administration, and other government-sponsored programs that operated, and others that continue to operate, to keep African Americans out and to provide benefits for white people. They are shocked to learn that so many towns and cities all over the United States have a history that has persisted well into this century as "sundown towns"—towns from which black people— on threat of violence—were, and often continue to be, excluded.[10] They are surprised to learn that residential segregation is not, as is often suggested, because people like to live with "their own kind," but is the result of a combination of restrictive covenants, redlining, and transportation designs that assured that the suburbs and particular urban neighborhoods were predominately, if not entirely, white. In short, the current situation of racial disparity is a result of a long and continuing history—one that many whites do not understand and that requires strenuous effort to confront.

This history is frightening because when we begin to explore it, we come face to face with a continuing history of racial violence. That the bedrock of our national wealth was built through a system kept in place by extreme levels of violence, including sexual violence, is hard to stomach.

And it brings us face-to-face with injustice of which whites are, by dint of history, an integral part. The fact that the violence continues today in new forms means that it cannot simply be brushed off as a thing of the past that doesn't concern us.

Whites are also afraid, I believe, of what it would cost to seriously commit to realizing racial equality—even though this would lead to a much healthier society for everyone. Clearly, repairing centuries of marginalization and exclusion comes with a high price tag. Resistance masks the shame involved in acknowledging the gross inequities of the current state of affairs and white complicity in them. Most white Americans are in fact well aware of the existing inequities; the knowledge is there, even if they have not been schooled in the historical facts; it is the commitment to racial justice that is lacking.

Another fear that is seldom talked about, but that lurks just below the surface, is the fear of retribution for the violence that has been a constant enforcer of racial injustice. In the recesses of many white people's imagination, African Americans are just waiting for the chance to get back at white people. When whites survey the enormity of the injustice, and consider how they would react if blacks had done this to them, there is a sense of foreboding. Whites need to face this fear head-on and to realize how much of it is based on their own projections. If we actually look at the record, it is astounding, given the levels of brutality and injustice inflicted on African Americans, how few incidents fit into the category of black people getting back at white people. Yet the fear is there; we hear it in jokes and humorous remarks that reveal the fixation.[11] Part of this is no doubt due to a sense of collective guilt. And perhaps part of it is because whites are so accustomed to seeing themselves as the central feature of all narratives. White people find it difficult to imagine that for others, they may be marginal to our country's equal opportunity story, except insofar as they interfere with it.

Finally, whites are afraid when they begin to grasp the immensity of the situation. They are afraid that this is impossible to fix, that the problem is just too big. Their pessimism in this regard is self-defeating and a refusal to assume power and responsibility for change. Are we shortchanging ourselves, underestimating our ability to make change? Ignoring the problem, pretending it doesn't exist, has never been an effective problem-solving strategy. Dr. King noted that Americans don't seem to have the same reservations when approaching other formidable challenges. The space program, for example, pushed the envelope of the impossible, and the country was willing to allocate huge sums of money to that challenge. All Americans should ask ourselves why the cause of racial equality here at home has not marshaled comparable enthusiasm and resources.

In 1968, Dr. King wrote these words: "America owes a debt of justice which it has only begun to pay."[12] Although forty-five years have passed, his assessment rings as true as it did then, Barack Obama's election and reelection notwithstanding. As a nation, we had in 1863, and in the years following, the chance to repair the damage wrought by slavery. Serious efforts were made by a small group of committed citizens, but there was never the political will necessary to see it through. We not only failed to repair the damages of slavery, we developed elaborate laws and practices designed to maintain white advantage—by any means necessary. These laws and practices ensured that the new citizens as well as their children and grandchildren would remain second-class citizens. We have had many chances since then to turn things around. Each time, we have failed to put in the kind of sustained effort required. And each time we have failed, the problem has gotten worse.

The effects of racial injustice are cumulative and build from one generation to the next. Once set in motion, racial inequality persists, morphing over time into new forms to fill the same function of conferring racial preference to one group at the expense of the others. If we think it will go away on its own, we are fooling ourselves. Racial inequality will not be eliminated until action is taken to reverse it. This is our challenge today, as it has been in the past. It is an enormous challenge that grows with each missed opportunity. The effort and resources required to establish racial justice in this country are significant. But now, as in the past, those resources do exist. And, as with each critical juncture in the past, the key deciding element will be people's commitment to making racial equality a reality. It will require major transformations, both personal and societal, and fierce determination. But it can be done.

Racial equality and justice will be set in motion when white people make and honor the commitment to join with African Americans and other racially marginalized populations to demand that our institutions change their preferential treatment by race—and when we are prepared to see that it gets done—at whatever cost. That's when it will happen.

A CHALLENGE FOR ALL OF US

For the evils of racism, poverty, and militarism to die, a new set of values must be born.
Martin Luther King Jr., *Where Do We Go from Here?*

The United States has become a society of vast social cleavages with a very small portion of the population controlling most of its wealth and the rest living increasingly precarious lives. At the same time, the growing preoccupation with national security continues to erode the basic freedoms that we hold dear. These changes make us a less stable society. As outlined in earlier chapters, economic and racial inequality have grown in recent decades. The security state, aided by new technologies of surveillance and control, is eroding personal freedoms at home and abroad. The long-standing War on Terror continues to sow justified resentment and bitterness abroad while policies that fuel social inequality create the same at home. The lack of widespread public debate about these developments is at least in part due to a growing fear of speaking out, and the belief that criticizing the practices and policies of the state is somehow unpatriotic.

One of the core values Dr. King exemplified in his life was civic engagement. He realized that justice is not something we attain and then sit back and enjoy; rather, it is something that must be fought for on a daily basis. A free and just society is a vigilant society. It requires a populace that is not afraid to look critically at its society, to call out injustice when they see it, and to hold their leaders accountable.

The imperative to challenge injustice is rooted in values of compassion and the ability to put oneself in another's place. Compassion serves as a guide in establishing and maintaining justice; without it, we cannot see beyond our own interests, nor can we see the ways in which our interests and the interests of others are related. Compassion demands that we act to defend the interests of others for the simple reason that we could easily be in their place. In a society that puts a high value on compassion, people look out for one another's interests. Compassion is a sort of insurance policy both for individuals and for society at large.

Compassion demands action and advocacy not only for the narrow rights of one's own group, but for the rights of everyone. This is the kind of action that, when strong enough and sustained enough, can push policy change. Without this kind of active advocacy, we cannot expect leaders to take action.

In writing this book, I have been struck by how far our society has moved away from the Beloved Community that Dr. King envisioned. We have grown into a society with deepening inequality, a highly militarized society, and one that remains profoundly racist. When Presidents Eisenhower and Nixon start to look like champions of civil rights, it is a sure sign that there have been some major changes in our collective state of mind. The crisis we face in the United States stems from a growing preoccupation with "security" and a situation of extreme economic inequality. Both have reached new heights and are intertwined with a deeply rooted system that confers advantage on white people while assigning blame to those it disadvantages. These factors interact in highly pernicious ways and correspond precisely to the Giant Triplets of militarism, materialism, and racism that Dr. King spent so much of his life warning us about. Like triplets, these forces are linked in complex ways. Their synergy makes it difficult to disentangle them and their effects. And because of this, the sum of their effects is more far reaching than any one of them might be alone.

Careful consideration of Dr. King's writings reveals a certain prophetic vision. We have turned away from Dr. King's messages of justice and chosen to follow a path of extreme materialism enforced by militarism both at home and abroad, with little regard for the human rights we talk so much about. We have become more divided economically and racially and more warlike. In short, we have moved away from rather than toward building the Beloved Community, a community grounded in justice and the notion that we are all connected, "tied together," as Dr. King said, "in the single garment of destiny."[13]

There are those who dismiss justice, compassion, and love as silly, idealistic notions—hardly worth serious consideration. They are seen as the domain of "bleeding-heart liberals," dreamers, and others who don't have a grasp of the real world. Values like greed, self-interest, and wariness are more often seen as the safest and most practical guides for living. After all, one never knows whether the next guy is out to get you. The "stand your ground" laws in force in twenty-two states as of this writing are a case in point. Their disparate application is another.

If there is a shortage of evidence that justice, compassion, and love are effective approaches, it is because they aren't used enough to test the hypothesis. No scientist worthy of the title would accept the paucity of evidence as conclusive. We have, however, tested the effectiveness of greed, self-interest, and suspicion of the other; the results speak for themselves.

The prescription Dr. King offered is one that may show us the way out of the current crisis, but it is not an easy one. It requires the birth of a new set of values. It demands that we rethink the deeply entrenched individualism that has guided us thus far and realize the complex ways in which we are interdependent, that the fate of the poorest and most marginalized among us affects us all. It requires critical thinking and, more than anything, commitment to the sustained work required to rebuild our society. It requires a certain kind of engaged patriotism—not just as Americans but as citizens of the world.

The militarism Dr. King warned about has only grown more deeply entrenched over the decades since his death. The United States has become even more arrogant and unethical in its international adventures. The stories of extraordinary rendition and revelations of torture in "black sites," images from Abu Ghraib, the systematic use of torture in Guantanamo, drone strikes on civilians in Pakistan, footage of U.S. military personnel urinating on the bodies of dead Afghanis, soldiers burning copies of the Koran—these are damning indictments of the War on Terror. A more apt title might be the War of Terror, as it continues to expand and spread fear and resentment throughout the world.

The military-industrial complex that President Eisenhower warned against in 1961 has grown out of control. Although there have been cuts in the defense budget, these are the result of larger economic constraints rather than any efforts to build a more peaceful world. Quite the contrary: we have become so warlike, so violent and arrogant in our interactions with others, that it will take a major overhaul of our national spirit to shift from the pursuit of war to the pursuit of peace. We have a long, long way to go. Whether we even start the journey will depend to no small degree on whether those of us who are fed up with continuing war insist on a new direction in our relations with the rest of the world.

At the same time, and in a not unrelated phenomenon, we are witness-ing unprecedented levels of militarism and surveillance domestically. This is justified, as is our international militarism, by the specter of terrorism, which our approach actually may be doing more to create than to thwart. The freedoms that we take such pride in are rapidly disappearing in the face of our drive to protect them from terrorists. If we do not wake up, they will soon be gone altogether. Is this what we really want?

Another of Dr. King's three major concerns was economic justice, the reasonable distribution of wealth and opportunity among the population so that no one need live in the grips of poverty. If, in the first decade after Dr. King's assassination, the nation seemed to be moving in the direction of economic equality, the years since then have found us going in the op-posite direction. Economic inequality has reached new heights, poverty rates have shot up, and there has been a shift in focus from who we *are* to what we *have*. We have perhaps lost sight of the fact that what we have is measured not so much by material goods but by a sense of belonging to an inclusive community that looks out for all of its members and makes their well-being a priority.

In spite of the enormous hopes pinned on President Obama, it has rapidly become clear that it takes more than a change in administration to change the direction of a nation. In the introduction to this book, I refer-enced the question posed by Vincent Harding in his 2010 introduction to *Where Do We Go from Here: Chaos or Community?* He asked, "Will Obama really see King?" I suggest again that an equally pertinent question may be whether the rest of us do, and if we are willing to reclaim the memory of Dr. King as a fierce advocate for justice who spoke truth to power and had the courage to resist the lure of easy violence. Dr. King urged us all to be courageous truth tellers and to take militant, massive nonviolent action to build a Beloved Community—something he believed was possible.

From this vantage point, some fifty years down the road from the March on Washington for Jobs and Freedom and the speech for which we remember him, I think of Dr. King's words toward the end of *Where Do We Go from Here?*: "In this unfolding conundrum of life and history there is such a thing as being too late."[14] Whether or not we are too late will depend crucially on our willingness to revive the memory of Dr. King's leadership and use it as a guide to action.

NOTES

Introduction

1. Martin Luther King Jr., *Where Do We Go from Here: Chaos or Community?* (Boston: Beacon Press, 2010 [1968]), 141.

2. Center on Budget and Policy Priorities, "Policy Basics: Where Do Our Federal Tax Dollars Go?" August 13, 2012, http://www.cbpp.org/cms/index.cfm?fa=view&id=1258.

3. 1968: 3.6%; 1982: 9.7%; 1983: 9.6%; 2010: 9.6%; 2011: 8.9%. Bureau of Labor Statistics, http://www.bls.gov/cps/prev_yrs.htm.

4. HUD report on homelessness, 2009, https://www.onecpd.info/resources /documents/5thhomelessassessmentreport.pdf.

5. Martin Luther King Jr.'s "I Have a Dream" address to the March on Washington, Washington, D.C., August 28, 1963, is available online at http://www.archives.gov/press /exhibits/dream-speech.pdf; audio of the speech is available at http://mlk-kpp01.stanford .edu/index.php/encyclopedia/documentsentry/doc_august_28_1963_i_have_a _dream/.

6. King, *Where Do We Go from Here,* xiv.

7. All quotes from Martin Luther King Jr., *Where Do We Go from Here: Chaos or Community?* (Boston: Beacon Press, 2010 [1968]), used with permission.

1. WHAT WE REMEMBER

1. For the maladjustment reference, see Dr. King's "A Look to the Future" address delivered at the Highlander Folk School, Monteagle, Tennessee, on September 2, 1957, mlk-kpp01.stanford.edu/index.php/encyclopedia/documentsentry/a_look_to_the _future_hfs/.

2. Martin Luther King Jr., *Why We Can't Wait* (New York: Harper & Row, 1964), 86.

3. The text of his acceptance speech can be read online at http://www.nobelprize.org /nobel_prizes/peace/laureates/1964/king-acceptance_en.html.

4. The full transcript of the trial is available at http://www.thekingcenter.org /civil-case-king-family-versus-jowers/.

5. The text of Dr, King's "Letter from Birmingham Jail," April 16, 1963, is available at http://mlk-kpp01.stanford.edu/index.php/resources/article/annotated_letter_from_birmingham/.

6. The text and audio files of President Kennedy's June 11, 1963, address are available online at http://www.americanrhetoric.com/speeches/jfkcivilrights.htm.

7. King, *Where Do We Go from Here?*, 3.

8. From Martin Luther King Jr., "The Other America," a speech given at Grosse Pointe High School, Detroit, Michigan, March 14, 1968. Text of the speech is available online at www.gphistorical.org/mlk/index.htm.

9. King, *Where Do We Go from Here?*, 21.

10. King, *Why We Can't Wait*, 87.

11. King, *Why We Can't Wait*, 86.

12. Dr. King's six principles of nonviolence and six steps of nonviolent social change are outlined on the King Center website in a document entitled "The King Philosophy," http://www.thekingcenter.org/king-philosophy. Briefly, nonviolence (1) is not passive, but requires courage; (2) seeks reconciliation, not defeat of an adversary; (3) is directed at eliminating evil, not destroying an evildoer; moreover, nonviolence entails (4) a willingness to accept suffering for the cause, if necessary, but never to inflict it; (5) a rejection of hatred, animosity, or violence of the spirit, as well as refusal to commit physical violence; and (6) faith that justice will prevail.

13. King, *Where Do We Go from Here?*, 58.

2. WHAT WE FORGET

1. King, "A Look to the Future."

2. www.dictionary.com.

3. King, "The Domestic Impact of the War," address to the National Labor Leadership Assembly for Peace, University of Chicago, Chicago, Illinois, November 11, 1967, text and audio http://www.aavw.org/special_features/speeches_speech_king03.html.

4. King, "A Look to the Future."

5. Martin Luther King Jr., "Loving Your Enemies," sermon delivered November 17, 1957, at the Dexter Avenue Baptist Church, mlk-kpp01.stanford.edu/index.php/encyclopedia/documentsentry/doc_loving_your_enemies/.

6. "The Social Organization of Nonviolence," *Liberation* 4, no. 5–6 (October 1959), available online through the King Papers Project at mlk-kpp01.stanford.edu/primarydocuments/Vol5/Oct1959_TheSocialOrganizationofNonviolence.pdf.

7. "Dr. King Is Winner of Nobel Award," *New York Times*, October 14, 1964, http://www.nytimes.com/learning/general/onthisday/big/1014.html#article.

8. King, Nobel Prize Acceptance Speech, University of Oslo, December 10, 1964. Full text and video links are online at http://www.nobelprize.org/nobel_prizes/peace/laureates/1964/king-acceptance_en.html.

9. Martin Luther King Jr., "Beyond Vietnam: A Time to Break Silence," address delivered at the Riverside Church, New York City, April 4, 1967, http://www.stanford.edu/group/King/liberation_curriculum/speeches/beyondvietnam.htm.

10. Ibid.

11. King, *Where Do We Go from Here?*, 193.

12. King, *Where Do We Go from Here?*, 193–194.

13. Ibid., 194.

14. Martin Luther King Jr., "The Quest for Peace and Justice," Nobel Lecture, University of Oslo, December 11, 1964, http://www.nobelprize.org/nobel_prizes/peace/laureates/1964/king-lecture.html.

15. Transcript of President Jimmy Carter's address at Lafayette College, April 2013, http://www.lafayette.edu/about/news/2013/05/08/transcript-of-jimmy-carters-speech-and-qa-session/.

16. Ibid.

17. King, *Where Do We Go from Here?*, 201–202.

18. Department of State and Other International Programs, Fiscal Year 2012, http://www.whitehouse.gov/omb/factsheet_department_state/.

19. Laicie Heeley, "U.S. Defense Spending vs. Global Defense Spending," Center for Arms Control and Non-Proliferation, April 24, 2013, http://armscontrolcenter.org/issues/securityspending/articles/2012_topline_global_defense_spending/.

20. David Wiley, "Militarizing Africa and African Studies and the U.S. Africanist Response," *African Studies Review* 55, no. 2 (September 2012): 147–161.

21. "In the councils of government, we must guard against the acquisition of unwarranted influence, whether sought or unsought, by the military industrial complex. The potential for the disastrous rise of misplaced power exists and will persist. We must never let the weight of this combination endanger our liberties or democratic processes. We should take nothing for granted. Only an alert and knowledgeable citizenry can compel the proper meshing of the huge industrial and military machinery of defense with our peaceful methods and goals, so that security and liberty may prosper together." Dwight D. Eisenhower, Farewell Address, January 1961, http://www.ourdocuments.gov/doc.php?flash=true&doc=90&page=transcript.

22. In the 1990s, Halliburton was found to be in violation of trade barriers to Iraq and Libya; its subsidiary KSG was accused of corruption by the Nigerian government, which it admitted. More on the record of Halliburton and subsidiaries, as well as Academi, can be found on the website of Corpwatch, http://www.corpwatch.org.

23. "What Iraq Taught Us about Reconstruction," interview by Kai Ryssdal for Marketplace, March 20, 2013, http://www.marketplace.org/topics/world/what-iraq-taught-us-about-reconstruction.

24. http://www.statisticbrain.com/u-s-war-death-statistics/ (data as of August 2, 2012).

25. Michael A. Fletcher, "Blacks Lose Ground in the U.S. Military: Unlike Vietnam, the Wars in Iraq and Afghanistan Have Not Accelerated the Progress of African-Americans to the Top Ranks," http://www.theroot.com/views/blacks-lose-ground-us-military?page=0,0.

26. "Veterans of Culturally Diverse Populations," *National Alliance on Mental Illness*, http://www.nami.org/Template.cfm?section=Multicultural_Issues.

27. "Iraq War: 190,000 Lives, $2.2 Trillion," March 14, 2013, http://news.brown.edu/pressreleases/2013/03/warcosts; "Iraq War 10 Years Later: Was It Worth It?" *Christian Science Monitor*, March 17, 2013, http://www.csmonitor.com/USA/Military/2013/0317/Iraq-war-10-years-later-Was-it-worth-it; "Iraq War Logs Reveal 15,000 Previously Unlisted Civilian Deaths," *Guardian*, October 22, 2010, http://www.theguardian.com/world/2010/oct/22/true-civilian-body-count-iraq; "More than 1,000,000 Iraqis Mur-

dered since 2003 Invasion," report on the Opinion Research Business Survey of 2007, September 16, 2007, Z-Net, http://www.zcommunications.org/more-than-1-000-000-iraqis -murdered-since-2003-invasion-by-orb.html.

28. From 2007 when UN first started reporting, to December 2012, civilian casualties in Afghanistan were estimated at 13,000. Susan G. Chesser for the Congressional Research Service, "Afghanistan Casualties: Military Forces and Civilians," December 6, 2012, http://www.fas.org/sgp/crs/natsec/R41084.pdf.

29. King, "Beyond Vietnam."

30. "Why I Am Opposed to the War in Vietnam," sermon at the Ebenezer Baptist Church, April 30, 1967, text, http://www.informationclearinghouse.info/article16183.htm; audio, http://archive.org/details/MartinLutherKingJr.whyIAmOpposedToTheWar InVietnam.

31. King, Where Do We Go from Here?, 184.

32. Ibid., 200.

33. Ibid., 67.

34. Ibid., 199.

35. The audio file of President Eisenhower's "Cross of Iron" speech can be accessed at http://archive.org/details/dde_1953_0416.

36. King, "The Domestic Impact of the War."

37. HUD figures, 2010, https://www.onecpd.info/resources/documents/2010homeless assessmentreport.pdf.

38. International Center for the Study of Prisons, 2010, http://www.prisonstudies.org /images/news_events/wpp19.pdf.

39. Adam Gopnik, New Yorker, January 2012.

40. Michael E. Martinez and Robin A. Cohen, "CDC: Health Insurance Coverage: Early Release of Estimates from the National Health Interview Survey, January–June 2012," http://www.cdc.gov/nchs/data/nhis/earlyrelease/insur201212.pdf.

41. "USDA Report Shows That Food Insecurity Remains High; More Than 50 Million Americans Face the Reality of Hunger," Feeding America, September 5, 2012, http:// feedingamerica.org/press-room/press-releases/usda-food-insecurity-2012.aspx.

42. February 21: Norcross, Ga.; February 27: Chardon, Ohio; March 8: Pittsburgh, Pa.; April 2: Oakland, Calif.; April 6: Tulsa, Ok.; May 30: Seattle, Wash.; July 20: Aurora, Colo.; August 5: Oak Creek, Wisc.; August 13: College Station, Tex.; September 27: Minneapolis, Minn.; October 21: Brookfield, Wisc.; December 11: Happy Valley, Ore.; December 14: Newtown, Conn.

43. King, Where Do We Go from Here?, 186.

44. King, "The Domestic Impact of the War".

45. King, Where Do We Go from Here?, 141.

46. Stockholm International Peace Research Institute, "The Top 20 Arms Exporters, 2008–2012, http://www.sipri.org/googlemaps/2013_of_at_top_20_exp_map.html.

47. United States Department of Defense Fiscal Year 2012 Budget Request, http:// comptroller.defense.gov/defbudget/fy2012/FY2012_Weapons.pdf.

48. For a discussion of the use of drones during the Obama administration and previous ones, see Peter Bergen and Megan Braun, "Drone Is Obama's Weapon of Choice," CNN Opinion, September 19, 2012, http://www.cnn.com/2012/09/05/opinion/bergen -obama-drone.

49. Jeremy M. Sharp. "U.S. Foreign Aid to Israel," *Congressional Research Service,* March 12, 2012, http://assets.opencrs.com/rpts/RL33222_20120312.pdf.

50. King, "The Domestic Impact of the War," address to the National Labor Leadership Assembly for Peace, November 1967, text and audio http://www.aavw.org/special _features/speeches_speech_king03.html.

51. King, *Where Do We Go from Here?,* 199.

52. Ibid., 68.

53. Ibid., 181.

54. "Child Hunger Facts," *Feeding America,* http://feedingamerica.org/hunger-in -america/hunger-facts/child-hunger-facts.aspx.

55. Laura Fitzpatrick, "The Minimum Wage," *Time,* July 24, 2009, http://www.time .com/time/magazine/article/0,9171,1912408,00.html#ixzz2IChaVOeN.

56. Available figures vary, 5 million being reported by Bloomberg in February 2012 ("Foreclosure Deal to Spur New Wave of U.S. Home Seizures, Help Heal Market," *Bloomberg.com,* http://www.bloomberg.com/news/2012-02-09/foreclosure-deal-to-spur-new -wave-of-u-s-home-seizures-help-heal-market.html), and 6.5 million reported by NBC News in May of 2011 (John W. Schoen, "Foreclosure Flood May Not Have Crested Yet," *NBCNews.com,* http://www.nbcnews.com/id/43099849/#.UWywtsqh6dY).

57. King, *Where Do We Go from Here?,* 199.

58. For calculations, see *MeasuringWorth,* http://www.measuringworth.com /uscompare/relativevalue.php.

59. A brief discussion of the FAP can be found at "Nixon," *The American Experience,* http://www.pbs.org/wgbh/americanexperience/features/general-article/nixon -domestic/.

60. King, *Where Do We Go from Here?,* 174.

61. King, *Where Do We Go from Here?,* 171.

62. Ibid., 138.

63. Ibid., 173.

64. Mel King, *Chain of Change: Struggles for Black Community Development* (Boston: South End Press, 1981).

65. King, "Beyond Vietnam."

66. "Conditional Cash Transfers: Reducing Present and Future Poverty," *The World Bank,* 2009, https://openknowledge.worldbank.org/bitstream/handle/10986/2597/47603 0PUBoCond101Officia10UseoOnly1.pdf?sequence=1.

67. These are inflation-adjusted 2010 dollars. World Bank, OECD figures. See United States—GDP per Capita: GDP per Capita (Current US$), *IndexMundi,* http://www .indexmundi.com/facts/united-states/gdp-per-capita.

68. "EITC and Other Refundable Credits," *Internal Revenue Service,* http://www.eitc .irs.gov/EITC-Central/abouteitc.

69. King, *Where Do We Go from Here?,* 199.

70. "Characteristics of Minimum Wage Workers: 2011," *Bureau of Labor Statistics,* http://www.bls.gov/cps/minwage2011.htm.

71. In this sense, programs like food stamps and other social supports might be most accurately seen not as "handouts to the poor" but as subsidies for employers who do not (and are not required to) pay living wages.

72. National Low Income Housing Coalition, www.nlihc.org. This site has an interesting calculator that shows how many hours per week at minimum wage you will have to work to afford specific rents.

73. Rebecca Thiess, "The Future of Work: Trends and Challenges for Low-Wage Workers," *Economic Policy Institute*, April 27, 2012, http://www.epi.org/publication/bp341 -future-of-work/#_ref2.

74. Kevin Phillips, *American Theocracy* (New York: Viking, 2006), 324–325.

75. Many of these speeches have been compiled by Michael Honey in Martin Luther King Jr., *All Labor Has Dignity*, ed. with intro. by Michael K. Honey (Boston: Beacon Press, 2011).

76. Martin Luther King Jr., speech to striking sanitation workers in Memphis, Tennessee, March 18, 1968. Full text is available online at http://www.aft.org/yourwork /tools4teachers/bhm/mlkpeecho31868.cfm.

77. Table 2. Median Weekly Earnings of Full-Time Wage and Salary Workers by Union Affiliation and Selected Characteristics, *Bureau of Labor Statistics*, http://www.bls.gov /news.release/union2.t02.htm.

78. Joseph Stiglitz, "Of the 1 Percent, by the 1 Percent, for the 1 Percent," *Vanity Fair*, May 2011, http://www.vanityfair.com/society/features/2011/05/top-one-percent-201105.

79. King, "A Look to the Future."

80. Steven Greenhouse, "Our Economic Pickle," *New York Times*, January 12, 2013, http://www.nytimes.com/2013/01/13/sunday-review/americas-productivity-climbs-but -wages-stagnate.html?_r=0.

81. Arloc Sherman and Danilo Trisi, "2011's Decline in Uninsured Is Largest in 13 Years, but Median Income Fell, Inequality Widened, and Poverty Stayed Flat," *Center on Budget and Policy Priorities*, September 17, 2012, http://www.cbpp.org/cms/?fa=view&id=3836

82. Emmanuel Saez, "Striking It Richer: The Evolution of Top Incomes in the United States (Updated with 2009 and 2010 Estimates)," March 2, 2012, http://elsa.berkeley .edu/~saez/saez-UStopincomes-2010.pdf.

83. Linda Levine, "An Analysis of the Distribution of Wealth across Households, 1989– 2010," *Congressional Research Service*, July 17, 2012, http://www.fas.org/sgp/crs/misc /RL33433.pdf

84. Thomas Shapiro, Tatjana Meschede, and Sam Osoro, "The Roots of the Widening Racial Wealth Gap: Explaining the Black-White Economic Divide," Brandeis Institute on Assets and Social Policy, Research and Policy Brief, February 2013. Available online at http://iasp.brandeis.edu/pdfs/Author/shapiro-thomas-m/racialwealthgapbrief.pdf.

85. Tax Policy Center, www.taxpolicycenter.org.

86. Greenhouse, "Our Economic Pickle."

87. Martin Luther King, Jr., "The Other America," Local 1199 Salute to Freedom, Hunter College, New York City, March 10, 1968. Full text appears in *All Labor Has Dignity*, ed. with intro by Michael K. Honey (Boston: Beacon Press, 2011), 165. A draft of the speech appears online at the King Center Archive: http://www.thekingcenter.org/archive /document/other-america; the quote appears on p. 17.

88. Erik Klineberg. "Adaptation: How Can Cities Be 'Climate-Proofed?," *New Yorker*, January 7, 2013, 32–37.

89. King, *Where Do We Go from Here?*, 51.

90. Ibid., 183.

91. Ibid., 95.

92. Ibid., 6.

93. Ibid., 51.

94. Ibid., 90.

95. Ibid., 84–85.

96. *Report of the National Advisory Commission on Civil Disorders* (New York: Bantam Books, 1968). A summary of the Kerner Commission report can be accessed at http://www.eisenhowerfoundation.org/docs/kerner.pdf.

97. Kerner Commission report summary, 1.

98. There were always a small number of Africans (and African descendants) who were free, indentured or otherwise. Though these individuals and families also did not get a fair share, it is important to know that historically most blacks were aware of this minority, if not a part of it.

99. King, *Where Do We Go from Here?*, 101.

100. King, *Where Do We Go from Here?*, 12.

101. King, *Where Do We Go from Here?*, 4.

102. But not so many: among the Fortune 500, there are only six black CEOs. See Chris Isidore, "African-American CEOs Still Rare," *CNNMoney*, March 22, 2012, http://money.cnn.com/2012/03/22/news/companies/black-ceo/.

103. Whose numbers are actually declining. See Jack Stripling, "Survey Finds a Drop in Minority Presidents Leading Colleges," *Chronicle of Higher Education,* March 12, 2012, http://chronicle.com/article/Who-Are-College-Presidents-/131138/.

104. The Center for Disease Control and Prevention (CDC) tracks racial disparities for a number of conditions. Their website is an excellent source of data on this issue: http://www.cdc.gov.

105. For a discussion of this and further resources see http://www.unaturalcauses.org.

106. King, *Where Do We Go from Here?*, 92.

107. King, *Where Do We Go from Here?*, 51.

108. Barack Obama, address to the 99th Annual Convention of the NAACP, July 15, 2008. Full text available online at http://news.cincinnati.com/article/20080715/NEWS0108/307150002/.

109. Kristin Seefeldt, Gordon Abner, Joe A. Bolinger, Lanlan Xu, and John D. Graham, "At Risk: America's Poor during and after the Great Recession," School of Public and Environmental Affairs, Indiana University, January 2012, http://www.indiana.edu/~spea/pubs/white_paper_at_risk.pdf.

110. Tami Luhby, "Worsening Wealth Inequality by Race," *CNNMoney,* June 21, 2012, http://money.cnn.com/2012/06/21/news/economy/wealth-gap-race/.

111. Final report of the American Freedmen's Inquiry Commission to the Secretary of War, Office of the American Freedmen's Inquiry Commission, New York City, May 15, 1864, www.civilwarhome.com.

112. Derrick Bell, *Silent Covenants: Brown v. Board of Education and the Unfulfilled Hopes for Racial Reform* (New York: Oxford University Press, 2004), 96. (The quote is taken from Judge Carter's 1968 article in the *Michigan Law Review* 67, no. 2, "The Warren Court and Desegregation.")

113. Matt Cover, "Unemployment Rises for Women, African-Americans in December," January 4, 2013, *CNSNews,* http://cnsnews.com/news/article/unemployment-rises-women-african-americans-december.

114. U.S. Census Bureau, "Income, Poverty, and Health Insurance Coverage in the United States: 2010," http://www.census.gov/prod/2011pubs/p60-239.pdf.

115. Adam Edelman, "Wealth Gap between Blacks and Whites Triples since 1984: Study," *New York Daily News,* February 27, 2013, http://www.nydailynews.com/news /national/black-white-wealth-gap-triples-25-years-article-1.1275422.

116. Michelle Alexander, *The New Jim Crow: Mass Incarceration in the Age of Colorblindness* (New York: New Press, 2010).

117. Vicky Pelaez, "The Prison Industry in the United States: Big Business or a New Form of Slavery?" *Global Research,* January 31, 2013, http://www.globalresearch.ca /the-prison-industry-in-the-united-states-big-business-or-a-new-form-of-slavery/8289.

118. Stephanie Ewert and Tara Wildhagen, "Educational Characteristics of Prisoners: Data from the ACS," presented at the Annual Meeting of the Population Association of America, Washington, D.C., March 31–April 2, 2011, http://paa2011.princeton.edu /papers/111587.

119. R. Coley, and P. Barton, *Locked Up and Locked Out: An Educational Perspective on the U.S. Prison Population"* (Princeton, N.J.: Educational Testing Service, 2006).

120. Ian Buruma, "Uncaptive Minds," *New York Times,* February 20, 2005, http://www .nytimes.com/2005/02/20/magazine/20PRISON.html.

121. Christian Henrichson and Ruth Delaney, "The Price of Prisons: What Incarceration Costs Taxpayers," *Vera Institute of Justice,* January 2012 (updated 7/20/12), http:// www.vera.org/pubs/special/price-prisons-what-incarceration-costs-taxpayers.

122. A 2013 report by the Centre for Research on Globalization cites IBM, Boeing, Motorola, Microsoft, AT&T, Wireless, Texas Instrument, Dell, Compaq, Honeywell, Hewlett-Packard, Nortel, Lucent Technologies, 3Com, Intel, Northern Telecom, TWA, Nordstrom's, Revlon, Macy's, Pierre Cardin, and Target Stores, among those benefiting from convict labor in private prisons. Pelaez, "The Prison Industry in the United States."

123. See prisoner report on working for Matori Farms (a supplier of Walmart) in Sadhbh Walshe, "How US Prison Labour Pads Corporate Profits At Taxpayers' Expense," *Guardian,* July 6, 2012, http://www.guardian.co.uk/commentisfree/2012/jul/06/prison -labor-pads-corporate-profits-taxpayers-expense.

124. John Tierney, "For Lesser Crimes, Rethinking Life behind Bars," by *New York Times,* December 11, 2012, http://www.nytimes.com/2012/12/12/science/mandatory -prison-sentences-face-growing-skepticism.html?partner=rss&emc=rss&pagewanted=a ll&_r=0&buffer_share=30230&utm_source=buffer.

125. Marc Mauer, Sentencing Project, congressional testimony, 2009, http://www .sentencingproject.org/doc/dp_cracktestimonyhouse.pdf.

126. Christopher Uggen and Sarah Shannon, "State-Level Estimates of Felon Disenfranchisement in the United States, 2010," *Sentencing Project,* July 2010, http:// sentencingproject.org/doc/publications/fd_State_Level_Estimates_of_Felon _Disen_2010.pdf.

3. WHY IT MATTERS

1. King, *Where Do We Go from Here?,* 94.

2. Ibid., 79.

3. Ibid., 93.

4. Ibid., 95.

5. Ibid., 71.

6. Ibid., 71.

7. Ibid., 10.

8. Ibid., 88.

9. James Baldwin, *The Fire Next Time* (New York: Dial Press, 1963), 19.

10. See James W. Loewen, *Sundown Towns: A Hidden Dimension of American Racism* (New York: Touchstone, 2005).

11. See, for example, Louis CK, "On Being White," http://www.youtube.com /watch?v=TG4f9zR5yzY.

12. King, *Where Do We Go from Here?*, 116.

13. King, "Letter from Birmingham Jail."

14. Ibid., 202.

JENNIFER J. YANCO was born in Boston and raised in
the Pacific Northwest. She holds a PhD in linguistics from Indiana
University and an MS in health and social behavior from the Harvard
School of Public Health. She served two terms as a Peace Corps
volunteer—in Congo and in Niger—and was a Fulbright lecturer in
linguistics at the University of Niamey. She has taught in the African
languages program at Boston University and for the past ten years has
served as Executive Director of the West African Research Association.
She lives in the Boston area, where she is a visiting scholar at Boston
University.

In 1999, in an effort to follow Malcolm X's advice that white people
work to fight racism in their own communities, she developed and
began teaching an adult education course, White People Challenging
Racism: Moving from Talk to Action. Over the past fifteen years the
course has been taught by an ever-expanding group of instructors and
continues to draw a wide range of students, both in the Boston area and
elsewhere in the United States.

Misremembering Dr. King is her effort to revive the memory of Martin
Luther King Jr. for current and future generations.